History of the Prust Family

With Stories From 1150 A.D England

By

Jeanette Prust-Smallwood

DEDICATION

In loving memory of my dear father, Bill Prust, 1926-2011.

This is a lasting tribute to the ancestors who have long departed this mortal life, giving them a touch of immortality!

And Dedicated to All the Prust descendants far and wide!

This family history I have written.
From an early age in our Great Britain,
From priests to pirates and lots in between
I started out searching how I came to be me.

These ancestors who made our history, so I am told
As I try to tell their stories as they unfold.
I found members of Landed Gentry abound,
Then others, struggling through life to turn it around.

It takes all sorts to make a world' so the saying goes.
Experiences in their life of their highs and their lows
Their happiness, joy, and their pain
We feel these emotions just the same.
We all have now, one thing in common
Hoping that one day we will not be forgotten!

ACKNOWLEDGEMENT

Thanking my cousin Simon Mills for his help in proofreading this book.

Thanking all the members of the Prust clan who gave their stories and photographs for use in this book.

Thanking the staff at 'The Mayflower Visitors Centre at Halfpenny Pier in Harwich for their information on the Mayflower.

Thanking Mr. Chris Keher of New South Wales, Australia, for his assistance in the early editing of this book.

PREFACE

Having always been interested in my family's history, I began researching my Prust side many years ago. I remember my grandfather telling me stories about his forebears, including how we were related to Guy Fawkes; so, as a child, every November 5, I told my school friends that the guy they were burning was my relation! Later, and with the internet at my disposal, I disproved this as another one of my grandfather's tales! However, there was an element of truth in the tale, as our ancestor was, in fact, on the other side as a parliamentarian; and was instrumental in helping to uncover the Gunpowder plot! And there is even a parchment within the family to prove this. Because of my early interest in our ancestors, my grandmother drew me a little family tree going back to just one generation. Little did I know that years later, with the help of the internet, BDM indexes, and trips to North Devon and Bristol, I would go on to find out some exciting and interesting facts about these ancestors, and with the help of information and documents from people here and around the world, I have written this book. These are historical events and stories of one of the most ancient families of Devonshire, 'The Prust Family of Hartland.' I have included stories about them that I hope may be of interest to you, the reader. The Prust family have been residing at Hartland, in North Devon, from at least the 1200s; their origins before this are not at all clear, and whether they were of Norman or Anglo-Saxon descent is open to debate. Locally, the name is sometimes PRIEST, and in West Country dialects, even Prist or Preest. I have endeavoured to try and give the feeling of the era in which these people led their lives, so I have included some historical events that happened in their lifetimes.

ABOUT THE AUTHOR

Jeanette Prust Smallwood was born in the East End of London in 1946. She was elected as a local councilor for the London district of Stepney in the 1980s and later moved to Essex with her husband, where she ran a wholesale plant nursery. She has been researching her family history on and off since the 1970s before the internet began, which later helped her to reach out across the globe and obtain stories from the descendants of people with this name. She is an accomplished painter and writer of poetry.

CONTENTS

Dedication.................... ii
Acknowledgement.................... iii
Preface.................... iv
About the Author.................... v
Introduction.................... 5
The Village of Hartland.................... 7
Hartland Parish Map.................... 10
The Prust Family And The Reformation.................... 11
Hartland Abbey.................... 12
The Dynham Survey of Hartland.................... 17
St Nectan's Church, Hartland, Devon.................... 18
The Visitation of the County of Devon.................... 22
The Visitation Translation.................... 24
The Squirearchy.................... 24
The Meaning of the Visitation.................... 25
The 'Prust Book of Hartland'.................... 27
Thomas and Thomasine Prust and Their 8 Children.................... 35
Will Of Judeth Prust of Nottacott 1615-1676.................... 38
The Three-Generation Gap.................... 40
The Middle Classes in Medieval England.................... 43
Descendants:.................... 44
Hartland Manor House.................... 46
- Old Disc found at Hartland a Monk's Calendar?.................... 46
- Hartland Money.................... 47
- Continuing: The Visitation from the Fifth Generation.................... 48

The Prust Family and the Ship 'The Mayflower'.................... 51
- More about the Ship and its Captain.................... 52

Hugh Prust of Goven II 56
Offspring of Hugh Prust of Goven II and Ann Carnsewe. 57
Hugh Prust of Monkleigh 1584–1666 60
Ann Carey, the Wife of Hugh Prust 60
Hugh Prust and Elizabeth Coffin/Coffyn 61
Prust V Pincombe 62
Prust Families of Hartland in the 17th-18th Century 74
Thomas Prust - A Case of Bigamy 78
Daniel Prust * 1827-1905 84
A Change of Name to Prust 87
Bartholomew Prust and the Ship Hms Bellophon 89
Hartland: Prust's Plot at High Farford 96
Stephen Prust of Bristol 1771-1850 97
The Slave Trade and 18th-19th Century Bristol 103
Prust Families Of Yorkshire 106
The Prust Families of Pembrokeshire Wales 111
Prust Family of Westleigh, Devon 116
Lily the Suffragette 122
William Prust 1847-1927 and Ellen Addams 1846-1927 124
Robert Prust 1874-1954 126
William Prust of Bristol 1781-1845 Jane Escott 1788-1852 129
Bristol 19TH Century 134
Mary Ann Prust 1818-1893 Charles Adams Bush 1806-1881. 136
Jane Prust 1822-1894 Joseph Drew 1819-1885 138
Stephen Prust 141
The Tailor 141
Caroline Prust 1824-1876 144
William Thomas Prust 152
Francis James Polkinghorn Pascoe' 161
Henry Pascoe 162

The London Prust's 165
William Edward Pascoe Prust 165
Frederick Octavious Prust 172
Theophilus Issiah Prust 174
William Edward Prust 175
William Edward George Prust 183
The Children of Bill and Ada Prust 186
Ethel Clara Cecilia Prust 1898-1974 191
Florence Laura Prust 1900-1986 192

INTRODUCTION

There are many lines of this once historic and famous family who were once regarded as 'Gentry' and married into noble houses to retain and enhance their wealth. It is thought that a 'Prust' came from Normandy with 'William the Conqueror' in 1066, though this is open to debate. What is known, however, is that all English people with the surname of Prust are descended from a small family group resident in the village of Hartland, in North Devon, since 11 99.

According to the Doomsday Book, Hartland (then known as Hertitone) was formerly owned by Gytha, Countess of Wessex, the mother of King Harold of England, who was defeated by William the Conqueror. The Doomsday Book records that in 1086 Hartland had "sixty villagers, forty-five smallholders, thirty slaves" together with plough land, "meadows 10 acres" and "woodland 12 acres" and "137 cattle, 50 pigs, 700 sheep, and 100 goats."

Boasting one of the finest coastal stretches in Britain, Hartland is home to 'Hartland Abbey,' which was founded by Gytha, King Harold's mother, and Hartland Quay, first constructed in the 15th-century harbour built by the monks of the Abbey.

The nearest villages to Hartland are Clovelly and Woolfardisworthy, and the local town is Bideford, where most of the birth, marriages, and deaths were recorded in church registers.

Here are some authentic accounts of England's Landed Gentry and of the families which have settled and lived in England or emigrated to start a new life in other parts of the world. They have grown with the national expansion and have primarily contributed to its greatness and glory, which has been preserved through successive generations and through all the political and socio-economic evolution.

The Prust family was to remain seated at Gorven in Hartland over the centuries, branching out to include employment with several Kings, three members of Parliament, two Abbots, and many merchants, ministers of religion, seafarers, and military officers.

Much of the historical information I have gathered will be of particular interest to readers of this surname and those with Prust ancestors who would like to know where they came from. They were from the social class of the Landed Gentry, which was the untitled aristocracy of England. They were a class with no hereditary titles but inherited landed estates passed on from generation to generation. In some instances, from the period of the Norman Conquest, they held a prominent place in many English Counties. A right of arms, sometimes of remote antiquity, served to supply a hereditary dignity. This is a frequent rallying point around which various members of the family are united.

THE VILLAGE OF HARTLAND

The origins of the Prust family lie in a village called Hartland in North Devon. Hartland was an early Anglo-Saxon estate mentioned in King Alfred's will, while its name was also given to the hundred in which it was situated. The largest Manor in this parish was held by the Dynham family from soon after the Norman conquest of 1066 until 1501. It was this family that founded and was a patron of the abbey at Hartland in 1169; they replaced the college of twelve canons that was mentioned in the Doomsday Book. They were, for several centuries, a leading family of the gentry in the county. The first record of the Dynham's holding land in Devonshire is a charter of 1122 of Geoffrey, lord of Dinan or Dyman in Brittany, recording gifts to the monks of two manors he possessed in England by the gift of King Henry the first.

In 1199 Oliverus de Dynham gifted 2 furlongs of land at Gorven to Osbert Prust, son of Richard Prust. It is not known if this was in addition to land already held by him or if it was a new agreement, perhaps as a gift in the way of a reward, as Richard Prust was at the time attached as a Canon to the Holy House at Stoke.

Today, Hartland is a large parish of approximately 17,000 acres. It is bordered on the west and north sides by the Atlantic Ocean. Hartland's remoteness from the chief highways of the Kingdom no doubt helped to preserve the parish from plague and other epidemic diseases.

Daniel Defoe wrote an interesting description of the economy of Hartland in 1724, most of which appears to be accurate.

"The town of Hartland which stands just within the shore is on the utmost edge of the county of Devon is a good market town, though so remote, and of good resort too, the people coming to it out of Cornwall, as well as Devonshire.... the seaman goes on shore here and supply themselves with provisions; nor is the town unconcerned in the great gainful fishing trade, which is carried on for the herrings on this coast, many seamen and fishing vessels belonging to the town".

(Source: Part of a Dissertation of the Social Structure of Hartland by Michael J L Wickes 1979-80. [27])

The coastline around Hartland is hard and rocky, a graveyard for ships through the ages. In the late sixteenth century William Abbot of the Manor of Stoke, St Nectan's in Hartland constructed a small quay about half a mile west of the church at Hartland. This Quay was swept away by the sea in 1818, and the pier wall again in 1887. It is recorded in church accounts that it was a thriving little port before its demise. It must have been difficult landing cargo at Hartland Quay, as the following sailing instructions dating from 1810 make clear:

"The back of the sea is exposed to a terrific sea, which, with southerly winds, causes a violent run inside. To sail in, keep head half a mile offshore until the pier bears SSE half E, and then run in" (Source: Part of a Dissertation of The Social Structure of Hartland by Michael J L Wickes 1979-80. [57])

Hartland Point Lighthouse gives a guide to vessels of all types approaching the Bristol Channel; the lighthouse was built by Trinity House in 1874 under the direction of Sir James Douglass. Built on a large rock at the tip of the point, the lighthouse was threatened by the undermining action of the sea to such an extent that rock had to be broken from the cliff head behind the lighthouse to fall on the beach and form a barrier against the waves. Unfortunately, this procedure had to be repeated at frequent intervals as the deposits were washed away whenever a North-Westerly gale coincided with a high spring tide. Eventually, it became necessary to construct a permanent barrier and a sea wall 30 metres long and 6 metres high, built in 1925.

Prior to automation in 1984, the station was manned by four keepers, who lived in dwellings attached to the lighthouse with their families. The dwellings were demolished when the station was de-manned to allow for the construction of a helipad next to the tower. Today the lighthouse is monitored from the Trinity House Operations and Planning Centre at Harwich in Essex. In 2012 the lighthouse building was sold, and the light exhibited from an alternative structure with the lighthouse building remaining a significant daymark.

HARTLAND PARISH MAP

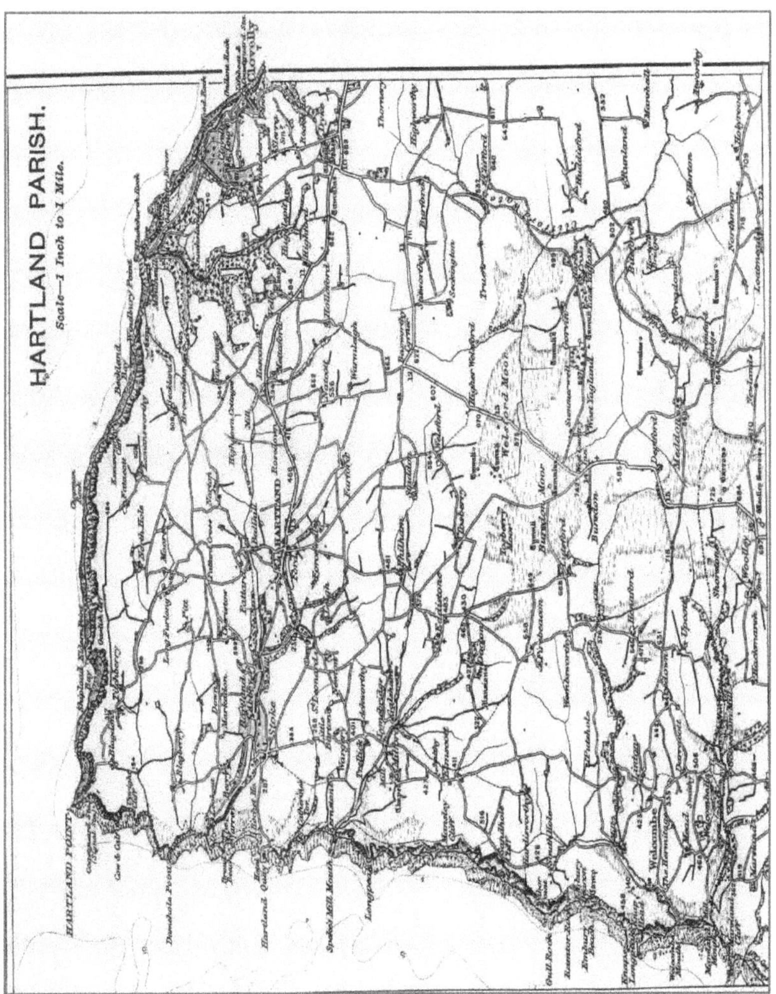

Ordinance Survey map of 1927

THE PRUST FAMILY AND THE REFORMATION

Henry VIII 1509-1547

The Reformation in the 16th century was based on Henry VIII's desire for an annulment of his marriage to his first wife, Catherine of Aragon. In 1533 the English Reformation was, at the outset, more of a political affair than a theological dispute.

During the Reformation, some of the Prust family refused to give up their old ways of worship (Catholic) to become Protestants, so their lands were confiscated. Despite this, some of the Prust family still stayed in and around the neighbourhood of north Devon.

Much later in the 18th century, Edmund Prust of Clovelly in Devon is found living there as a 'Steward' to Colonel Paul Orchard, who then owned Hartland Abbey through his marriage to the Lutterell family. Edmund Prust was not the first member of this family to reside at Hartland Abbey, as earlier in the 16th century, two cousins named John Prust were Abbots of The Abbey.

HARTLAND ABBEY

The foundation of Hartland Abbey was through a gift of Lord Dynham, lord of the Manor of Hartland and a representative of the Norman family who took over this area after the Norman Conquest in **1066.** The Abbey is situated near Hartland Point in an area of outstanding natural beauty in the northwest corner of Devon. It lies in a wooded valley only one field wide, which runs inland from the wild and precipitous Atlantic coast - a coast that was both revered and feared by generations of seafarers and where the local wreckers plied their deadly trade. The Abbey was built in the twelfth century and consecrated by Bishop Bartholomew of Exeter in A.D.**1160** as a monastery of the regular canons of the order of St. Augustine of Hippo, to serve St. Nectan's Church, Stoke, which is the Parish Church of Hartland.

Prust Abbots in Hartland Abbey

There were two Abbots (cousins) who were both members of The Prust family. The elder **John Prust,** with his convent, became Abbot in **1462** and granted in **1523** to John Chamond, esquire for his good counsel on us bestowed an annuity of twenty shillings payable out of the Manor of Launcells, and in 1527 he leased to Thomas Hunt clerk, and Robert Dey the Rectory of Knowstone at a rent of 8/-. He died in the summer of **1529** and was succeeded by **John Prust, junior,** as Abbot on August 21, **1529.** This prior election was notified on August 18, **1529,** to the patrons and founders, John Fitzwarren, John Zouche, and John Arundell, Knights, who were representatives of the Dynham family. Three days later, he made his profession of obedience to the see of Exeter in the chapel of the Virgin Mary within the church. In March of that year, he and the convent appointed Thomas Arundell Esquire head steward of all the abbey property in Devon and Cornwall and elsewhere. These Arundells were distinguished men: Sir John

Arundell was the son of Lord Dynham's sister Catherine, and Thomas, Sir John's second son, was afterwards knighted and married a sister of Queen Catherine Howard, who was beheaded in **1553.**

The second Abbot, **John Prust,** had very little peace during his years in office. In **1531**, in the reign of King Henry VIII, Abbot John Prust of Hartland Abbey was forced to institute proceedings in the 'Star Chamber' against eight persons who came to Hartland in a manner of war, and with swords, daggers, staves, and other invasive weapons they terrorised the community. These persons, upon hearing of the proceedings brought against them by John Prust, formed a gang and decided to take the law into their own hands and teach John Prust a lesson. In retaliation, they broke open the doors of the residence of John Prust at the Abbey and proceeded to assault, menace, and threaten his life. There was little help for Abbot John Prust as soon after, in **1533,** the King decided to break away from Rome and make England a protestant country; this was the start of 'The Reformation.'

In 1534, The Abbot, with five of his canons, acknowledged the Royal Supremacy, but by now, an old man was already a marked victim of Thomas Cromwell, who was known as "*the hammer of the monks.*" [1]

Thomas Cromwell, who was the first Earl of Essex, was an English statesman who served as the chief minister of King Henry the VIII. Cromwell was one of the strongest advocates of the English Reformation and helped engineer an annulment of the King's marriage to Catherine of Aragon so that Henry could marry his mistress, Anne Boleyn.

1. Letters and Papers of Henry VIII, VII, No.1121(63)

Later that same year, Thomas Cromwell and the bishop of Exeter appointed a joint commission for the visitation of all abbeys and Royal Catholic religious houses. This royal commission was for visiting commissioners to uncover sexual immorality and financial impropriety amongst the monks and nuns. However, in fact, it was to value their assets with a view to expropriation.

One of the visiting commissioners was Sir William Courtenay of Powderham. Sir William wrote in one part of his report, commenting against Abbot John Prust as follows:

"With the chancellor of Exeter, and Richard Pollard, I have been at the Abbey of Hartland and examined the convent on diver articles. I find there are great causes of deprivation against the said Abbot and convent. The Abbot has no learning sufficient to rule and I had so much laughing at the Abbot's examination. I never saw such a foolish priest, for he confessed more things against himself than we examined him upon. Interest was made for him by Sir Thomas Arundel who was there as his special friend for which reason I send you this letter."
(Source: Letters and Papers of Henry VIII appendix No.37)

(Note: Sir William Courtenay was the Sheriff of Devon and the 2nd Great Grandfather of Thomasine Courtenay, who married Thomas Prust of Hartland in about 1600.)

A few days after the above report, the "good and just Sir Thomas Arundel" wrote his report and, together with his father, Sir John Arundel, wrote this letter on Abbot John Prust's behalf. This is a small exert of the letter <u>for</u> the Abbot stating:

"That it is not true that the abbot has no wit or has wasted the goods of the house. The house is in very good case, and this man is most fit and there is no blot on his morals".
(Source: Letters and papers of Henry VIII No.38)

History tells us that Henry VIII was going to order the closure of the wealthy Roman Catholic monasteries and convents and later did that. The Arundel's tried to reinstate the old Abbot by force and failed as Sir William Courtenay appointed two justices of the peace to eject the old Abbot successfully.

So it came to pass that on February 23, **1536**, Thomas Pope was appointed to be the next Abbot, together with his convent. He was more of a 'Caretaker' Abbot and was well prepared for the dissolution of the Abbey and convent and set about making money for himself. He at once began to grant leases of the abbey property and annuities and offices to his friends. It is said that he also conveyed away the valuable plate of the house. Knowing that the Reformation was about to happen, he granted **Henry Prust** and his wife Katherine for a cash payment of one hundred shillings a part of Barton of Stoke in the parish of Hartland for 16 years paying yearly one grain of corn (a peppercorn rent).

Meanwhile, both Thomas and John Arundel petitioned for an annuity (Pension) for the Abbot, and in **1536** John Prust was awarded only 40 marks = £26.13s.4d for the term of his life. The old Abbott John Prust died in **1545**. This a short excerpt from his will including misspelt words:

I give to Hugh Prust of Gorven, a coffer, a chair, in my chamber a flock bed, a pair of sheets, a coverlet, a bolster, a cushion, a basin of pewter, a broad pewter dish, a sucer, two mass books, a alter towel, a holy water bucket and a pair of cruets. To each of my sisters Joane Yeo, Elizabeth Yeo, and Katherin Kingsland to each of them a new hat covered in taffeta. To two little children which be of my sister to each of them a little hat. To Sir Wm. Dyngley, clerk, and Sir John Williams clerk, 3s.4d each.

Signed: Johannem Prust.

The end came for the Abbey and monastery when in February of 1539, the surrender of the abbey and all its possessions was signed. Thomas Pope was granted a pension of £66.13.4d, a much larger sum than the poor Abbot John (Johannem) Prust.

Some of this information came from 'The Book of Hartland' by R. Pearce Chope (1862-1938), edited by Isobel Thornley, lecturer in History at University College, London and published in 1940. It is no longer available in print, though a limited facsimile edition was printed in 1995.

The end of this true story is that the persecutor of our John Prust, Thomas Cromwell, who was a government minister, fell out of favour with King Henry the VIII. Whereupon Thomas Cromwell was accused of treason, and without trial, he was executed on Tower Hill in the year **1540**.

After the death of Henry the VIII, our defender of John Prust, Sir Thomas Arundel (who was at the time one of the most influential officials in England), met the same fate. It is known that a conspiracy was formed against him with unproven allegations. It was said by his enemies that he was still devoted to the old religion (which he was said to be a practising Catholic), and there was concern that he could have an influence on the young son of Henry VIII, King Edward the VI. Although protesting his innocence, Sir Thomas Arundel was arrested and charged with trying to overthrow the government. He was convicted and beheaded on Tower Hill in the year **1552** and met the same fate as Thomas Cromwell. Capital punishment at the time was beheading which was reserved for the upper classes instead of the usual method of hanging for ordinary people, even for a minor offence.

THE DYNHAM SURVEY OF HARTLAND

The Dynham survey of 1566 covers a large section of the parish and lists freeholdings on the Dynham Manor with the names of tenants and the amount of rent paid. It also gives customary holdings and Barton tenancies, with tenant names, the amount of rent paid, and the acreage of arable, meadow, and moorland held by each tenant. The land was held on a system of leases for three lives. In practice, many of these tenancies were held during four lives since the name of the actual tenant is invariably different from the three names accompanying it. There were records of the existence of four granary mills on the Dynham manor alone, leading to speculation that the borough was self-sufficient. The land was mainly arable farming, with some given over to pasture for grazing, mainly for sheep. The farmers of Hartland may have had access to rough grazing on Burresdon Moor as the Dynham survey records show that **Sir John Perrot 1527-1592** (portrait left) held the Barton tenancy of Burresdon Moor with a rent of six shillings and ten pence which was such a low rent for three tenancies even in those days. The celebrated Sir John Perrott was Lord Deputy of Ireland, who inherited these tenancies from his wife **Jane Pollard** nee **Prust.** She was the daughter and heiress of **Hugh Prust of Thorvey,** who was a gentleman, and who owned two free tenancies there at Burresdon Moor, now called Bursdon Moor. Jane first married Sir Lewis Pollard of Kings Nymton in Devon; he died before 1569, and by whom she had three children. Sometime after Jane was widowed, she married Sir John Perrott and had a further three children by him, William, Ann, and Lettice Perrot. Sir John Perrot was rumoured to be the illegitimate son of King Henry VIII. When Jane died in **1568,** Letters of Administration of her estate were granted to Sir John Perrot (knight). Interestingly Sir John Perrot later died in The Tower of London. He was accused of high treason, this might have been a trumped-up charge as Queen Elizabeth was ruthless in her rule, especially with favourites in her father's reign. Sir John Perrott was found guilty! But sentencing was put off for some months in the hope of a royal pardon, although this was uncertain. It is believed that Sir John Perrot was murdered in the Tower, having been poisoned in anticipation of his release.

ST NECTAN'S CHURCH, HARTLAND, DEVON.

The Prust family of Hartland worshipped at Hartland church which stood in the hamlet of Stoke and was the former Abbey church despite its position being two miles west of the Borough of Harton, in Stoke.

Hartland church, now called St. Nectan's, was named for a Celtic missionary who was the eldest son of the Welsh King Brychan of Brycheiniog in south Wales. He was a hermit and, seeking solitude, ended up in a remote valley in Hartland. In about 510 AD., robbers stole his cows, and in trying to get them back, he was killed. His tomb is near the site of the church. It is situated at Stoke near the Quay so that passing ships can see its majestic tower. Saint Nectan is the Patron Saint of Hartland. St. Nectan Church (shown above) was founded in **1050** by Gytha, the Countess of Wessex and the mother of King Harold of England.

In the church of Saint Nectan's, there is a Prust family pew (pictured). It was erected in the south chapel and was commissioned with the initials HP engraved and set in its own shield at either end of the pew. There were a few ancestors named Hugh Prust during the 16th and 17th centuries, although **Hugh Prust of Goven** was the church treasurer of St Nectan's in 1613. It is believed that he commissioned this pew and gave the pew ends to Sant Nectan's Church. For more about Hugh Prust of Goven, see page 49.

Many Prust family members were baptised and married in the church and buried in the churchyard of this beautiful church.

There is an interesting story from about **1615** regarding Squire, Lord of the Manor Luttrell, and Thomas Prust regarding a curate who was employed by a new institution called 'Charterhouse,' previously a rectory in Hartland.[1] The first curate who was appointed by Charterhouse was William Churton; this curate made himself particularly obnoxious to Squire Luttrell of the Abbey, whose charge against him amounted to this: *that he had set himself to base and servile labour such as fetching home sand in his cart for manuring the ground, refusing to baptise children, or to administer the Sacrament to dying parishioners, not reading the Litany, but administering Communion to excommunicated persons;* a true rebel of the church indeed, or maybe he was in the wrong profession! It was confirmed by Thomas Prust that in a certain sermon, he said the following: *That if Papists and Protestants did marry together, they brought forth mongrels, nay were Atheists*, and in another sermon, he was quoted as saying, *"Where god hath the Church, the devil hath the chancel"* referring to Mr. Luttrell. Churton was known to be a quarrelsome man, threatening and reviling his neighbours, calling them Abbey lubbers, rascals, puppies, reprobates, etc. Churton was acquitted of these charges as he was buried as a "minister" in 1646.

1. Source: The Book of Hartland by R. Pearce Chope.

A pew list of **1613** found in Hartland Church records shows the position of everyone depending on economic or social status, which goes to show an interesting model of the social structure of the parish in that era. This list shows that the gentry and the wealthy or yeomen sat in seats near the chancel while women and males of inferior status sat towards the west end of the church. Andrew Lutterell, Lord of Stoke Manor, was in pride of place in the chancel. **James Prust** gent was placed in the north chapel. The main value of the pew list lies in its representation of social power in Hartland parish. Gentry, farmers, and the inhabitants of Harton borough were well represented because renting a church pew was seen as a mark of social prestige and could only be done for a price. The wealthier members of the parish occupied a large proportion of the limited number of seats. The first seat was allotted to **Hugh Prust of Goven,** who would be sitting in his pew at the head of the south side of the church; his wife sat behind him with other notable women. It will be seen that although generally men and women had separate seats, they were intermingled, but there seems to be a tendency to put men in the front and women behind. The blue dots in this seating plan represent a male parishioner, and the pink dot represents a female parishioner.

In a prime position in this seating plan is Andrew Luttrell, Lord of the Manor of Hartland; he was in the top section 2, row 2, seat number 1.
Hugh Prust of Goven sat at the front in section 10, Row 1, seat No.1.
James Prust of Southole was seated in Section 3, row 2, seat No. 2.
George Prust (Gov. of goods) of Lutsford was also seated in section 3, row 3, seat No.1
John Prust (Church Warden) was seated at the side in section 6, row 2, seat No.1.
Thomas Prust of Notcott (gov. of goods) was in section 9, row 2, seat No.4.
William Prust was a wine grower in agriculture, and he was seated in section 9, row 3, seat No. 4.
By contrast, **Mrs. Hugh Prust** (Ann Carnsewe) was seated in section 9, row 8, seat No. 3 and **Mrs George Prust** (Anna Down) was also seated in section 9, row 5, seat No. 4, a long way back from their husbands.

Note: The principle adopted usually seems to have been to place them as far apart as possible by the church authority. The 1613 pew list shows that the puritan idea of the 'family pew' had not reached as far as Hartland. The congregation was firmly divided into male and female groups, with a few exceptions, and wives were usually separated from their husbands. The farming community certainly formed a large proportion of the congregation in 1613.

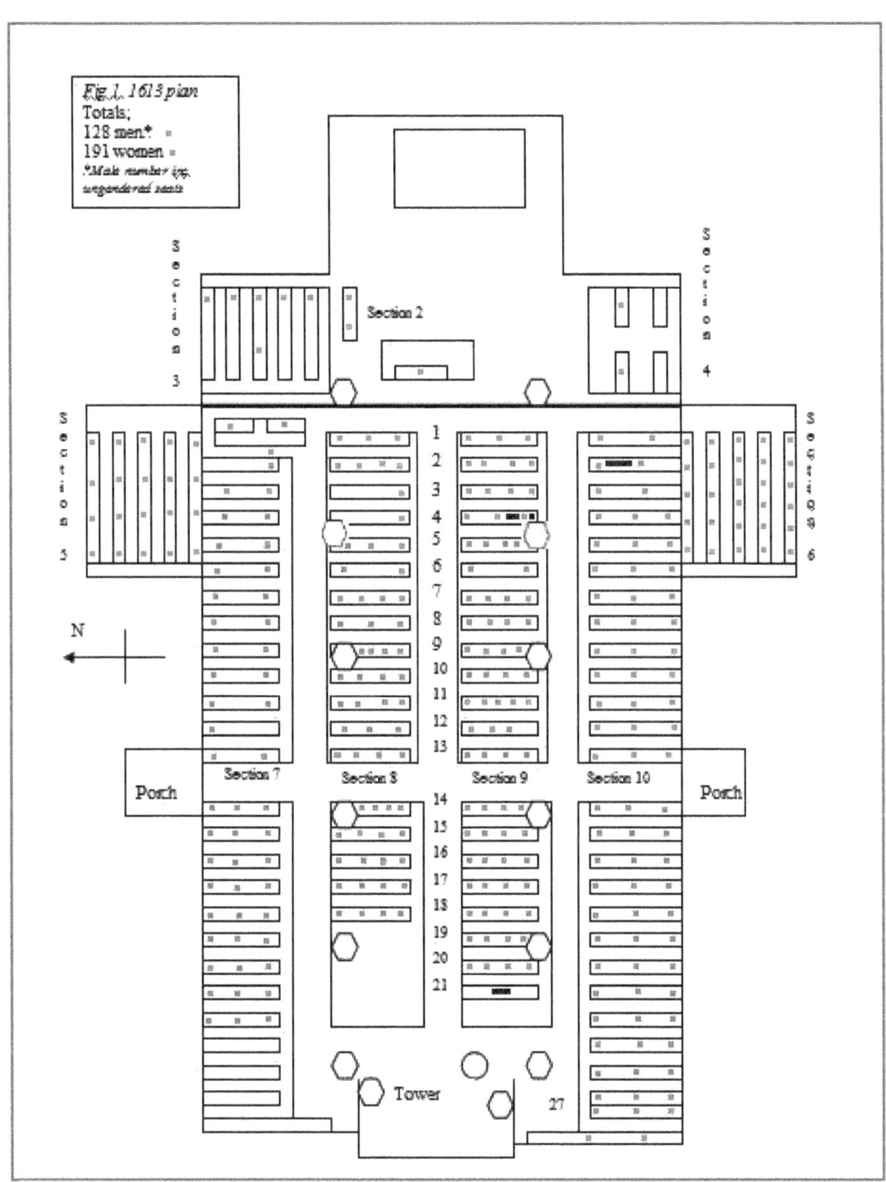

Fig.1. 1613 plan
Totals;
128 men*
191 women
Section 2
Section 3
Section 4
Section 5
Section 6
Section 7
Section 8
Section 9
Section 10
N
Porch
Porch
Tower
1
2
3
4
5
6
7
8
9
10
11
12
13
14
15
16
17
18
19
20
21
27

THE VISITATION OF THE COUNTY OF DEVON

Prust.

Oliverus de Dynam temp. Reg. Johannis a° 1199 dedit Osberto filio Ricardi pro homagio et servicio suo duos furling. terræ in Gorven.

Johannes Holman de Gorfen dedit et concessit Thomæ filio suo omnia messuagia terras et tenementa sua in Gorfen. Dat. anno regni regis Ricardi 2 decimo nono.

Petrus Cobin et Tho. Judd dederunt et concesserunt et per cartam suam confirmaverunt Johannæ nuper uxori Tho. Holman omnia messuagia, terras et tenementa sua cum pertenentiis in Gorfen quæ nuper habuerunt de dono et feoffamento Tho. Holman, habend. et tenend. omnia predicta messuagia prefatæ Johannæ ad terminum vitæ suæ remanen. Agnete filie eorum Tho. et Johanne et heredibus suis in perpetuum. Dat. apud Gorfen nono Octob. quarto H. 6.

Robertus Prust per cartam suam dat. 11 die Feb. 15 H. 6 dedit omnia messuagia sua in Southole in hund. de Hartland Johanni Prust filio juniori dict. Roberti et heredibus de corpore predicti Johannis junioris remanere Johanni Prust seniori filio suo dicti Roberti et heredibus de corpore suo exeuntibus, remanere Balwino Prust 2 filio dicti Roberti et heredibus de corpore suo procreatis remanere Johanni Prust de Gorven et heredibus suis in perpetuum.

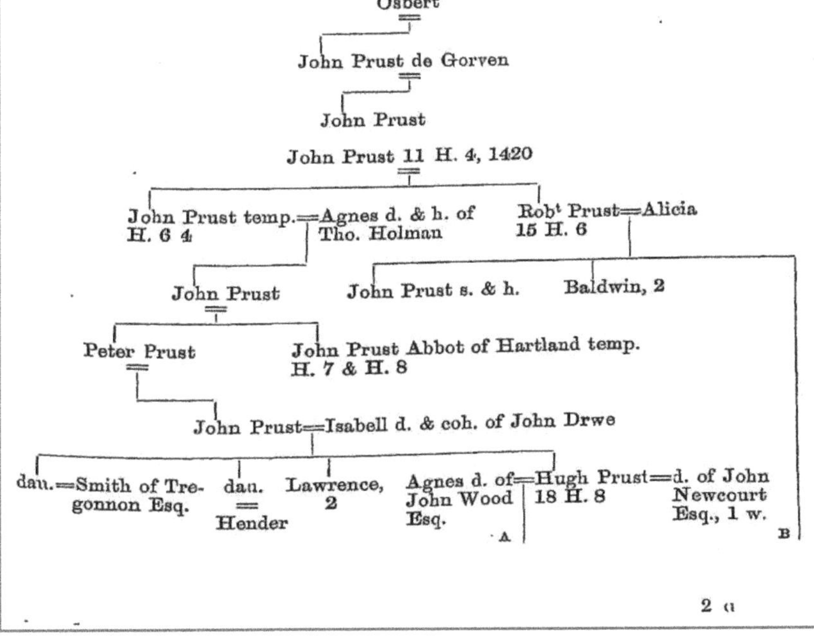

2 G

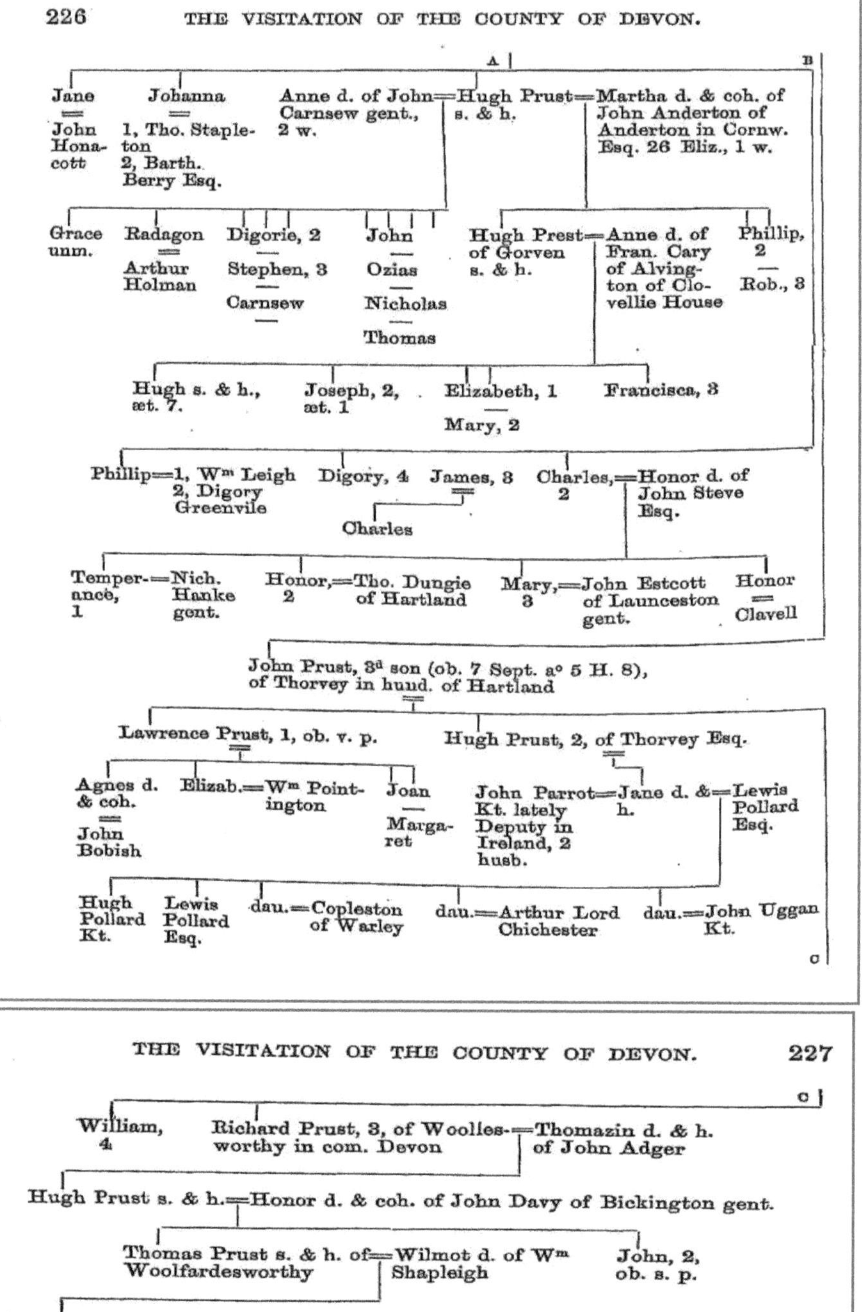

226 THE VISITATION OF THE COUNTY OF DEVON.

A | B

Jane = John Honacott

Johanna = 1, Tho. Stapleton 2, Barth. Berry Esq.

Anne d. of John Carnsew gent., 2 w. = Hugh Prust s. & h. = Martha d. & coh. of John Anderton of Anderton in Cornw. Esq. 26 Eliz., 1 w.

Grace unm.

Radagon = Arthur Holman

Digorie, 2 — Stephen, 3 — Carnsew —

John — Ozias — Nicholas — Thomas

Hugh Prest of Gorven s. & h. = Anne d. of Fran. Cary of Alvington of Clovellie House

Phillip, 2 — Rob., 3

Hugh s. & h., æt. 7.

Joseph, 2, æt. 1

Elizabeth, 1 — Mary, 2

Francisca, 3

Phillip = 1, Wm Leigh 2, Digory Greenvile

Digory, 4

James, 3 = — Charles

Charles, 2 = Honor d. of John Steve Esq.

Temperance, 1 = Nich. Hanke gent.

Honor, 2 = Tho. Dungie of Hartland

Mary, 3 = John Estcott of Launceston gent.

Honor = Clavell

John Prust, 3d son (ob. 7 Sept. aº 5 H. 8), of Thorvey in hund. of Hartland =

Lawrence Prust, 1, ob. v. p. =

Hugh Prust, 2, of Thorvey Esq. =

Agnes d. & coh. = John Bobish

Elizab. = Wm Pointington

Joan — Margaret

John Parrot Kt. lately Deputy in Ireland, 2 husb. = Jane d. & h. = Lewis Pollard Esq.

Hugh Pollard Kt.

Lewis Pollard Esq.

dau. = Copleston of Warley

dau. = Arthur Lord Chichester

dau. = John Uggan Kt.

C

THE VISITATION OF THE COUNTY OF DEVON. 227

C

William, 4

Richard Prust, 3, of Woolliesworthy in com. Devon = Thomazin d. & h. of John Adger

Hugh Prust s. & h. = Honor d. & coh. of John Davy of Bickington gent.

Thomas Prust s. & h. of Woolfardesworthy = Wilmot d. of Wm Shapleigh

John, 2, ob. s. p.

Thomas Prust s. & h. = Thomazan d. of Roger Courtney of Ottrey St. Mary Esq.

Thomas Prust s. & h., æt. 6, 1620

William, 2

Richard, 3

Katherin, 1 — Ulalia, 2

Margaret, 3

Entered, not signed.

THE VISITATION TRANSLATION

The following is a translation (from the original Latin) of the beginning of THE VISITATION OF THE COUNTY OF DEVON, which mentions some of the Prust family from the 12th century to the 17th century.

Oliver of Dynam in the reign of King John in the year 1199 gave to Osbert, the son of Richard, for his homage and service, two furlongs of land at Gorven.

*John Holman of Gorven gave by charter (I think this also could be by will or endowment) to his son Thomas all the buildings, land and tenancies that were his at Gorven. Dated in the 19th year of the reign of King Richard II (*which would have been 1396)

Peter Cobin and Thomas Judd by deed and charter confirmed that Joan the wife of the late Thomas Holman is possessed of all the houses, land, and tenancies together with all the chattels and stock at Gorven that the late Thomas Holman had and left to his wife Joan for the rest of her life; and then it is to pass to their children, their daughter Agnes and their sons Thomas and John and to their heirs in perpetuity. Dated this October 9 in the 4th year of the reign of King Henry VI. (Which would have been 1426).

Robert Prust by charter (or will) on the February 11 in the 15th year of the reign of Henry VI (so in 1437) gave all of his property and houses situated at Southole in the hundred of Hartland to John Prust his youngest son and heir; as John the first son, and Baldwin the second son, had died without issue, leaving his youngest son John Prust of Gorven and then to his heirs in perpetuity.

THE SQUIREARCHY

The Oxford English Dictionary defines 'squirearchy' as the collective body of Squires, landed proprietors or country gentry, but a more exact definition would be the collective body of squires or esquires, persons legally entitled to bear heraldic arms. Armorial bearings are or should be the outward sign of the rank of 'Gentility', the lowest hereditary rank, and only persons able to prove legitimate descent from the grantee have any rights to use them. They visited Hartland in 1531, 1664, and 1620 and recorded the following six families of gentry: Abbott of Hartland and Luffincott, Cholwin of Lutsford, Docton of Docton, Luttrell, **Prust of Gorven**, and Velly of Hartland, and at a later date, Stucley, Orchard, and Wolferstan were also armigerous families.

These are the two coats of arms used by members of The Prust Family.

Arms: A Black shield with two black Estoiles on a silver chief. The later edition of a coat of arms was used with three red Estoiles on a silver chief with the crest of a Black Martlet. (This signifies a heraldic Swallow, which is a bird perceived as swift and elegant, it also signifies nobility acquired through bravery, prowess, or intelligence.)

THE MEANING OF THE VISITATION

The heraldic visitations were tours of inspections undertaken by the King of Arms on behalf of the King. Their reports were important and gave the right for family to bear their coat of arms in England, Wales, and Ireland. This was to regulate and register the coat of arms of nobility, the gentry, and boroughs and to record pedigrees. They first took place in **1531**, during the reign of King Henry VIII, and another in **1564** and again in the reign of Elizabeth I up unto the last one in **1620,** in the reign of King James I.

By the fifteenth century, the use and abuse of coats of arms were becoming more widespread. One of the duties conferred on the principal King of Arms by the reigning monarch was to survey and record the armorial bearings and pedigrees of those using the coat of arms and to correct irregularities. The officers of the King of Arms of England made occasional tours of various parts of the country in order to enquire about armorial matters. By the sixteenth century and under a warrant from Henry VIII, this process was carried out in earnest. The then King of Arms, Thomas Benolt, was given authority to enter all homes and churches and to deface at his discretion or 'put down' any arms that were unlawfully used. He was also required to enquire into all those using the titles of knight, esquire, or gentleman and to decide if they were lawfully used.

The mayors and sheriffs of each county were ordered to assist the officer of arms in the task of giving aid and gathering information. The people that were using titles or arms were summoned to the Visitation, and the hope was that none would escape the enquiry. They were ordered to give proof of their right to use these arms, and their ancestry was duly recorded. When an official grant of arms had been made, this was recorded, and many of these predated the establishment of the College of Arms. The Visitations were not popular with the landed gentry, who were required to present proof of their gentility. In 1689, William III of Orange and Mary II came to power, and the visitations ceased.

The Visitation was confirmed and carried out in **1620** with the added children of **Thomas Prust** and **Thomasine Courtenay**. (line C of the tree) was the direct descendant of King Edward l through his daughter Princess Elizabeth Plantagenet down to a member of the famous Courtenay family of Powderham Castle in Powderham, Devon. Princess Elizabeth Plantagenet married twice; her first husband was John 'Count of Holland', who died soon after their marriage. Her second husband was Humphrey de Bohun, also known as the 4th Earl of Hereford and the 3rd Earl of Essex, whom she married in **1302** and by whom she went on to have ten children. One of those children, a daughter, was born in **1311** and was known as **Lady Margaret de Bohun**, she was betrothed to **Hugh de Courtenay** from an early age, and they married in **1325** when she was 14 years old. Margaret and Hugh had 13 children together, and through the male line, the generations went down to Thomasine Courtenay, daughter of Roger Courtenay, Esquire of Ottery St. Mary in Devon.

Thomas Prust and his wife Thomasine Courtenay had six children, Thomas, William, Richard, Katherine, Margaret and Ulalia Prust; they were all the 13th direct descendants of King Edward I. Sadly, I am unable to find the descendants of these six children. Their lines of descent may have died out, or perhaps there was a change of name, and no documentation exists. I could find nothing further, BUT perhaps you might!

THE 'PRUST BOOK OF HARTLAND'

Front Cover below

This Prust book was about the Genealogy, including some history of The Ancient family of Prust of Hartland in Devon. It was commissioned by **Mr. William Aubrey Prust** in **1912**, over one hundred years ago, and undertaken by Mr. Richards of Stoke Newington in North London. He took on the enormous task of researching, writing and illustrating this book. He included his own sketches of the various coats of arms where no other means of copying them were possible. It must have taken him quite a long time to complete, as he had to get information from the various bodies, including The Heralds.

Mr. William Aubrey Prust was born in **1877** and was the 21st direct descendant of Richard Prust of Hartland **1150**. Mr William Aubrey Prust and his wife **Beatrice Grossmith** were planning on emigrating, and he wanted to leave a legacy in posterity for the next generations of the Prust family. The first pages that were written in this book are the following:

An authentic account of our landed gentry – of the families or family, which settled on the soil, have grown with the nation growth, and have principally contributed to its greatness and glory- which have preserved through successive generations and through all the charges of political convulsion and social progress, the manly high spirited and courageous character of the Anglo-

Saxon race must needs be important in the public point of view, and be of the highest individual interest.

The Landed Gentry the untitled Aristocracy of England is a class unexampled and unrivalled in Europe, invested in no hereditary titles but inheriting landed estates transmitted from generation to generation, in some instances from the period of the conquest and the Plantagenet's, this class has held and continues to hold a foremost place in each county.

A right of arms sometimes of remote antiquity serves to supply to want of a hereditary dignity and is the rallying point around which are collected the various members of the family.

Amongst the most ancient county families of Devonshire, is that of PRUST OF HARTLAND, where it has been seated for the long period of between 800 & 900 years.

Fifteen descents of this ancient race are traced in the "Visitation of the County of Devon" in AD 1620. GOVAN in HARTLAND was the old family seat, and there is resided from generation to generation, throwing out branches at Woolfardisworthy; Monkleigh etc., etc. The elder branches of the PRUSTS appear to have removed to NOTTICOTT, another estate in Hartland.

This book is an authentic account of the family of what was available to Mr. Richards at the time, bearing in mind that we now have much more at our disposal via 'the internet.' Also, there are better photographs available of various coats of arms, some of which I have included in this book.
The book, *The Ancient Family of Prust of Hartland* was left in the care of Mr. Michael Horace Prust of Hartland in Devon but is now in the care of his granddaughter, who still lives in Hartland. This book is not available online.

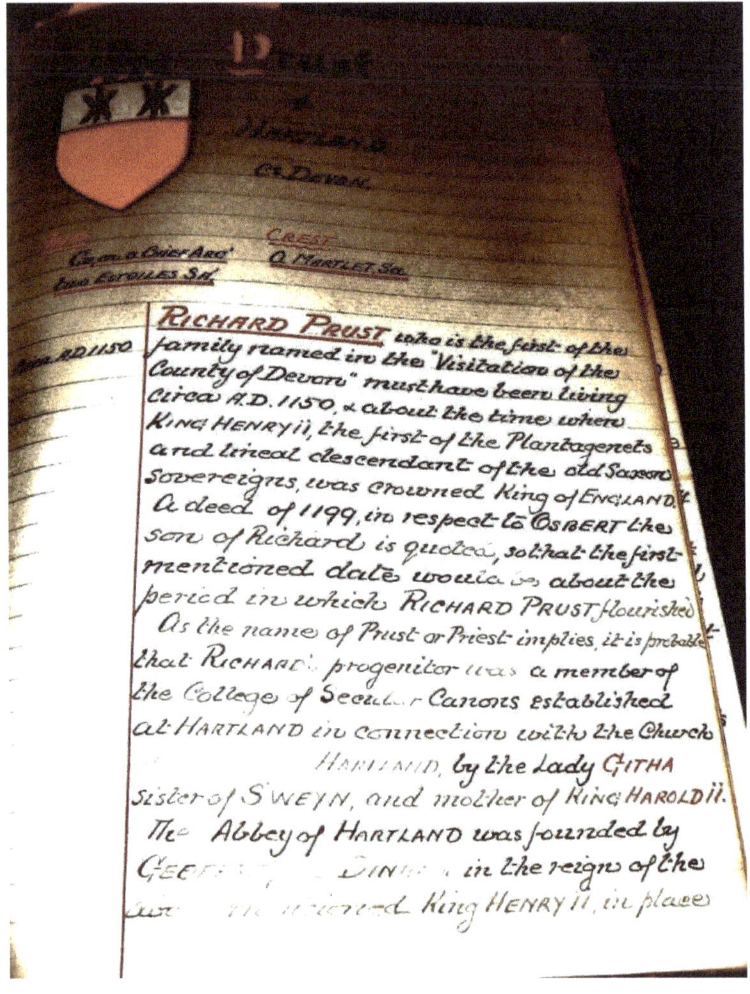

Prust of Hartland Co. Devon.

Gu. on a Chief Arg' two Etoilles Sa.

Crest: a Martlet Sa.

Circa A.D. 1150

Richard Prust who is the first of the family named in the "Visitation of the County of Devon" must have been living circa A.D. 1150, & about the time when King Henry ii, the first of the Plantagenets and lineal descendant of the old Saxon Sovereigns, was crowned King of England.

A deed of 1199, in respect to Osbert the son of Richard is quoted, so that the first-mentioned date would be about the period in which Richard Prust flourished.

As the name of Prust or Priest implies, it is probable that Richard's progenitor was a member of the College of Secular Canons established at Hartland in connection with the Church [illegible] Hartland, by the Lady Githa sister of Sweyn, and mother of King Harold ii.

The Abbey of Hartland was founded by Geo[illegible] D[illegible] in the reign of the [illegible] King Henry ii, in place

The last seven lines, which are unclear, read: The College of Secular Canons established at Hartland in connection with the church of St. Nectan, Hartland, by the Lady Githa (Gyntha) sister of Sweyn, and mother of King Harold ll. The Abbey of Hartland was founded by Geoffrey de Dynham in the reign of the above-mentioned King Henry II, in place.

[illegible] Richard Prust was succeeded by his son.

OSBERT PRUST of HARTLAND. He is named in a deed, the date being
Dte 1199. given 1199.
Unfortunately the deed quoted by the Herald does not now appear to be in evidence. It may exist in some private collection & possibly would throw some light as to what property the Prusts held & were connected with at this early date.—
Osbert PRUST was succeeded by his son & heir—

JOHN PRUST who was living temp'
circa AD 1250 King HENRY III (1216-1272) John Prust is the first to be styled "of GORVEN," one of the family estates so long held, in the parish of HARTLAND. Lysons' in his "Devonshire" (CLXXX-I.) seems to infer that the Gorven property was brought into the Prust through the heiress of the Holmans, some generations later than the above named John Prust 'de Gorven' as he is termed by the herald.
John Prust was succeeded by his son & heir

JOHN PRUST of HARTLAND. He may be identical with the John Prust or Prest who distinguished himself in the Kings foreign Wars & for such good services

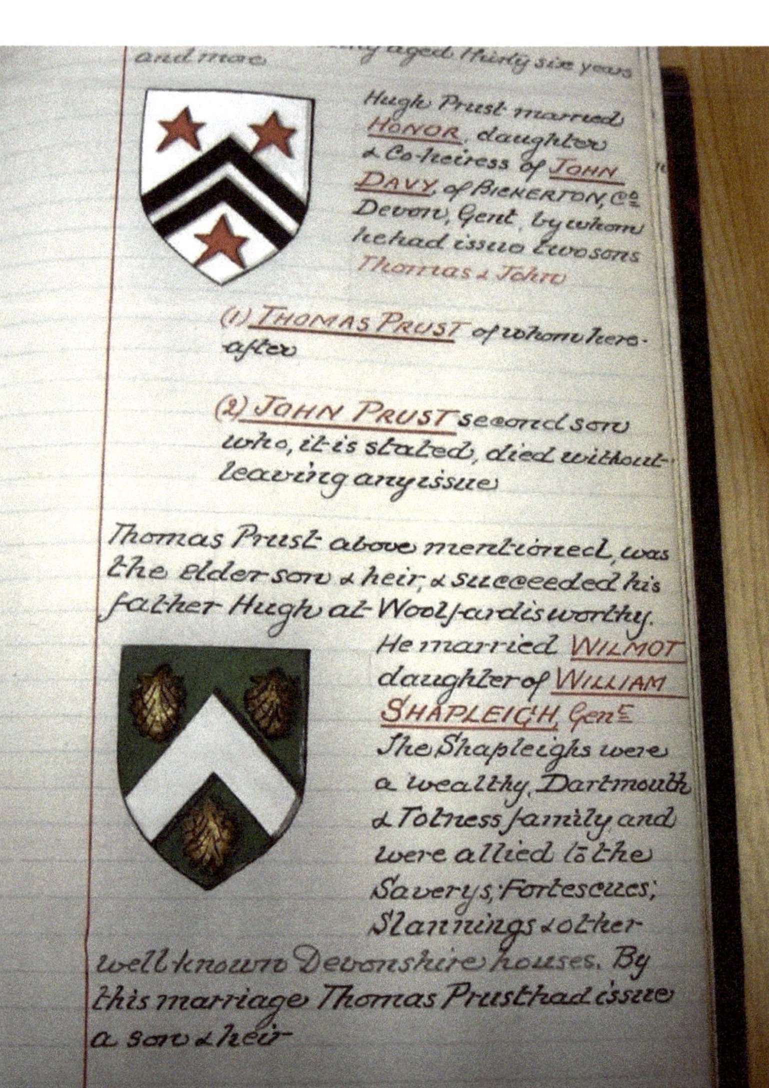

and mae [illegible] aged thirty six years

Hugh Prust married HONOR, daughter & Co-heiress of JOHN DAVY, of BICKERTON, Co. Devon, Gent, by whom he had issue two sons Thomas & John

(1) THOMAS PRUST of whom hereafter

(2) JOHN PRUST second son who, it is stated, died without leaving any issue

Thomas Prust above mentioned, was the elder son & heir, & succeeded his father Hugh at Woolfardisworthy. He married WILMOT daughter of WILLIAM SHAPLEIGH, Gent. The Shapleighs were a wealthy Dartmouth & Totness family and were allied to the Saverys, Fortescues, Slannings & other well known Devonshire houses. By this marriage Thomas Prust had issue a son & heir

THOMAS PRUST of WOOLFARDISWORTHY

19

Co Devon. He married THOMASINE daughter of ROGER COURTENAY Esquire of OTTERY St MARY, Co DEVON. This alliance with the great house of COURTENAY brought into the Prust family a Royal Descent from the HOUSE of PLANTAGENET, as follows:-

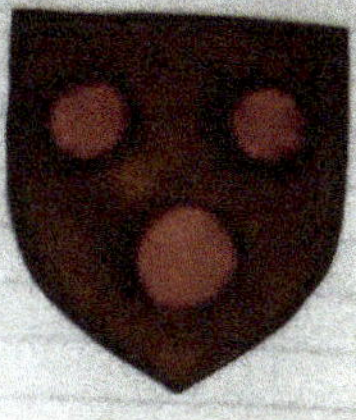

EDWARD Ist KING of ENGLAND, ob 1307 Son of King HENRY IIIrd of ENGLAND = ELEANOR, daugr of FERDINAND III KING of CASTILE.

BOHUN

(1.) Princess ELIZABETH PLANTAGENET, ob 5 May 1316 ae 32. = HUMPHREY de BOHUN Earl of Hereford & Essex, killed 1322

COURTENAY

HUGH de COURTENAY 2nd Earl of Devon b 1303, ob 2 May 1377, bur' in Exeter Cath: Kt of the GARTER. = Lady Margaret de BOHUN, m 31 Aug 1325 ob 16 Dec 1391, bur' in Exeter Cathl. (2)

(3) SIR Philip Courtenay KtG. 4 son. Of POWDERHAM Lord Lieut of Ireland. He d 29 July 1406. = ANNE, daugr of Sir Thomas Wake, Kt

SIR John Courtenay Kt. 2 son, died v.p. (4) = Joan, daugr of Alexander Champernoune Esq died 1419.

page 19.

No.	Courtenay line	Spouse
(5)	Sir Philip Courtenay Kt. of Powderham, Devon. Son & heir of Sir John & Lady Joan. He d. 16 Dec 1463	Elizabeth, daugr of Walter, Lord Hungerford K.G. she d. 14 Dec 1476.
(6)	Sir William Courtenay Kt. of Powderham son & heir: Sheriff of Devon 1483 & d. 1485	Margaret, daugr of Willm Lord Bonville
(7)	Sir William Courtenay Kt., of Powderham, son & heir d. 1512	Cecily, daugr of Sir John Cheyney Kt. of Pinhoe, Devon.
(8)	Sir William Courtenay Kt., of Powderham, son & heir Called "the Great" He d. 24 Novr 1535. Will proved 27 May 1541 P.C.C.	Mary, daugr of Sir John Gainsford 2 wife, By her will proved 12 Feb 1570 She gave all her property to her son John of Ottery St Mary.
(9)	John Courtenay of Ottery St Mary, Co Devon, Had all his mother's property 1570	Thomasine, daugr & heir of Nicholas Huntingdon Esqr
(10)	John Courtenay of Ottery St Mary, only son	Mary daugr of ?
(11)	Roger Courtenay of Ottery St Mary (Visit of Devon 247 ebb)	Ann, daugr of ? Prust
(12)	William Courtenay; Thomasine Courtenay	Thomas Prust

See over for issue, page 20

Thomas Priest had by his wife the aforesaid Thomasine, daughter of Roger Courtenay three sons and three daughters all of whom through their mother would be 13th in descent from EDWARD 1st KING of ENGLAND 1272-1307. and it follows that the descendants of these children could also claim a descent from this great Plantagenet King.
The sons & daughters are as follows.

(1) THOMAS PRUST of whom here-after: (see page 31)

(2) WILLIAM PRUST, 2 son, named in the Will of his kinsman Hugh Preest Esq. of Monkleigh Devon, 1650

(3) RICHARD PRUST 3rd son.

(4) KATHERINE PRUST.

There was a further four daughters to Thomas and Thomasine Prust, namely: Ulalia Prust, Margaret Prust, Wilmot Prust and Elizabeth Prust.

The above records are taken from line 'C' of the Visitation of 1620 and from records detailed in the Will of Thomas Prust, the elder, who died in 1658. Obviously, there are many more lines to be explored to continue from what was provided to the Heralds at that time; and I have done that to bring us forward another generation. I will start, though, with some information on Thomas Prust and Thomasine Courtenay.

THOMAS AND THOMASINE PRUST AND THEIR 8 CHILDREN

Thomas Prust (**1585-1658**), son and heir of Thomas Prust and Wilmot Shapleigh, married a lady of great lineage. She was Thomasine, the daughter of Roger Courtenay of Ottery St Mary, in Devon.

The Prust (shown with only two estoiles at that time) and Courtenay coats of arms are shown below. (The later coat of Arms of the Prust family has three estoiles)

The Courtenay families of Powderham in Devon were wealthy, titled, and famous. And it would have been considered a great match to marry into the Courtenay family. It also shows the influence of the Prust family at that time.

Thomasine Courtenay was the 12th in descent granddaughter of King Edward I of England **1272-1307**. He was also known as Edward Longshanks and the 'Hammer of the Scots.'

Through the Courtenay female line, she traced descent from Princess Elizabeth Plantagenet, the daughter of King Edward I. Thomasine died in about **1642** and is buried in the graveyard of All Hallows Church in the village of Woolfardisworthy, east of Hartland in Devon. This village is where many of this family lived, died, and were buried.

1) The first son of Thomas and Thomasine was **Thomas Prust** (**1614 1675**). He was known as Thomas Prust of Nottacott. He was mentioned in the 1650 will of his relative Hugh Prust Esquire, Gentleman of Monkleigh in Devon.

This **Thomas Prust of Nottacott** married **Judeth Collings (1615-1676)** of Climsland (Climscott) in Cornwall. She was the daughter of George Collings Esquire and Elizabeth Mayor. The Coat of Arms of the 'Collings' family is shown left. Thomas and Judeth had eight children, and all were christened in Hartland, Devon. Their children were:

a) **Grace Prust** was baptised in **1636**. She married twice, first to **Robert Atkins** of Morwenstow in Cornwall in 1663 and then to **Joseph Corydon** in 1676, also in Morwenstow, Cornwall.

b) **Thomas Prust** baptised in **1637,** sadly died in 1640, aged just three years.

c) **Elizabeth Prust** baptised in **1640**.

d) **Judith Prust** baptised in **1642**.

e) **Margaret Prust** baptised in **1644**.

f) **Thomas Prust (1646 - 1674)** married **Ann Champneys**, daughter of John and Ann Champneys of Yarscome, Devon. They had a daughter named Anne Prust, who was baptised in May 1674, one month after her father died.

g) **Hugh Prust** (**1652-1669)** and

h) **h) Mary Prust (1654-1660).**

Thomas Prust (1585-1658), the Elder of Woolfardisworthy, died aged 74 in **1658.** His will on the next page gives us a snapshot of who he was, where he lived, and the family that survived him:

Will Of Thomas Prust of Woolfardisworthy 1585-1658

'In the name of Go Amen on the One and Twentieth day of October in the year of our Lord God according to the computation of the Church of England One thousand six hundred and fifty seven I Thomas Prust the elder of the Parish of Woolfardisworthy in the County of Devon, Gentleman being in good health and of a disposing mind and memory (Thanks be given to Aalmighty God for the same) I hereby revoke all former wills by me hereunto fore made and do make and ordain this my last will and testament in name and form following. First, I commend my soul to Almighty God my mournful Creator. And my body to a Christian burial. I give to the poor of the parish of Woolfardisworthy aforesaid Twenty shillings to be disposed by my executors in this my will hereinafter named. Also, I give to the poor of Clovelly Ten shillings. Also, I give and bequeath to my son Thomas Prust Twenty shillings and my gold ring wherein is my seal and Arms and also my chest wherein I dutifully have my writings. Also, I give and bequeath unto my son William Prust Twenty shillings. Also, I give and bequeath to my son Richard Prust Twenty shillings. Also, I give and bequeath to my daughter Katherine Stapledon Twenty shillings. Also, I give and bequeath to my daughter Ulalia Turbow Twenty shillings. Also, I give and bequeath to my daughter Margaret Bannio Twenty shillings. Also, unto my sons William Prust, and Richard Prust all my apparel to be equally divided between them. Also, I give to each of my grandchildren that shall be living at the time of my death and at any time born during my life ten shillings a piece. Also, I give unto my daughters Wilmott Prust and Elizabeth Prust all my messuages and close of land meadows and pay hire (parcels of one Tenement at Woolsey lying within the Parish of Woolfardisworthy aforesaid ...)

Thomas goes on to set out the terms of the Trust to give to his daughters Wilmott and Elizabeth, detailing the land and its names, that they are to pay a rent of 16 shillings a year to be collected at four feast days a year and to give his godchildren 12 pence apiece. He names his daughters Wilmott and Elizabeth as his Executrixes.

Then there is the will of Judith Prust (nee Collings) made in **1675**, the wife of Thomas Prust of Nottacott and the daughter-in-law of Thomas Prust, whose will is on the previous page. She left all her goods and assets to her four daughters and an annuity to her daughter-in-law Ann, the widow of her son Thomas. There were no sons alive at her death. Her will also give us an insight into the family. The will is transcribed with the same spelling as used in the 17th century, and as this document is extremely old, some parts are missing hence the xxxxx's

WILL OF JUDETH PRUST OF NOTTACOTT 1615-1676

In name of God Amen: I Judeth Prust of Nottacott within the parish of Hartland In the Countye of Devon widow being infirm of body, but of sound and perfect mind and memory (blessed be god) doo make and ordayne this my last will and testamentIn manner and form following; first I committ and commend my soule unto god who gave it and my body to the earth from whence it came to be decently interred when god shall transfer me home. Also, I give toward the repairation of the parish Church of Hartland aforsaid Twenty shillings. Also I give to the poure of the parish fourty shillings. Also I give and bequeath unto my daughter in law Anne Prust the widow and relict of my sonne Thomas Prust Late deceased twenty Shillings. Also I give unto my daughters Grace Atken widow, And Elizabeth Prust unto each of them Twenty Shillings. Also I give and bequeath unto my daughter Judeth Prust Twenty pounds of Lawful English money to be payd withyn one year next after my death. Also I give and bequeath unto my daughter Margarett Prust All my Right Estate Title form and interest what favour of me and to All the foresaid fourth parts of Two messuages and Tenements, and of Two half farthings of Land, and of one Close of Land with the appurtenances in Christowe, and one halfe farthing of Land in Youltree and one halfe farthing of land appurtenances in Norton and Corkisland and of one in the fourth parts of A cottage with appurtenances in Harton Mill being all parcels of the Manor of Hartland and sometimes reputed to be the lands of Edward Lord Zouth, and were ? unto ? in the tennure of Richard Deyman deceased, and are now hole and enjoyed by me and my assignes by right and venture of one obligation, whereby my said daughters Elizabeth Prust standeth bound unto me in the sum of one hundred pounds, with condition to xxxxxxxxx Executors Administrators Assignes quietly to have hold and Enjoy xxxxx in Morewenstow Youltree Norton Corksland and Hawton Mills during her life (as in and by the said obligations and condition ?lation to me then I unto more fully ?eth with said obligation with all the benefit and Advantages to be ?????? I give and bequeath unto my said daughter Margarett Prust. And all the residue of my goods and Chattels not formerly by me given and

This concludes the descendant tree from King Edward the 1st and the Prust family unless you know different! This concludes the line of 'C' of the visitation of 1620.
bequeathed I give unto my said daughter Margarett Prust whom I do make and ordayne to be the sole Executrix of this my Last will and Testament In witness whereof I have hereunto set my hand and Seale the eight days of April in the year of our Lord God one Thousand six hundred seventye and five in the presence of

Judeth Prust Loco Sigile

Note: Loco Sigile is Latin for 'In place of her signature.'

2) **William Prust,** the second son of Thomas and Thomasine, was born in about **1615** and was known as William Prust of Climscott, Hartland. He died in **1658**, aged 43 years old. No descendants have been found so far for William.

3) **Richard Prust**, the third son of Thomas and Thomasine, was born about **1618** and died and was buried at Hartland in **1690**. Richard married Joanne (surname unknown), and Richard and Joanne had at least four children.
Thomas Prust of Woolfardisworthy (1661-1708),
Katherine Prust
Susanna Prust
Jane Prust.
(All these children were baptised at Hartland in Devon, although no birth dates are given for the females).

4) **Katherine Prust,** daughter of Thomas and Thomasine, married a gentleman with the surname of **Stapleton.**

5) **Ulalia Prust,** daughter of Thomas and Thomasine, married a gentleman with the surname of Turbow/**Turnbow**

6) **Margaret Prust,** daughter of Thomas and Thomasine, married a gentleman with the surname of Bannio/**Banyo**

THE THREE-GENERATION GAP

As you may have noticed, there is at least a three-generation gap in the Visitation of 1620 between John Prust, who lived in about 1300 and John Prust II H.IV,**1410**. I believe I can fill in some of the histories. First, I think it worthwhile to give some biographies of a few notable Prust family members of the time.

John Prust of Hartland (shown in the Visitation), son of John Prust of Gorven, was born in about **1255**. He was mentioned in the patent rolls for distinguished service to the Plantagenet King, Henry III of England, for fighting in the wars. John had three sons Richard, Thomas, and Hugh.

Richard Prust was born about **1280** and went on to become a Member of Parliament. In 1307 Richard was returned as a member of the borough of Cornwall. Richard himself went on to have issue, two sons, Robert and William.

Robert Prust, who followed in his father's footsteps to become a Member of Parliament, representing Bodmin in the county of Cornwall; Robert also had two sons, Henry and John.

Henry Prust who was a Naval Commander and Member of Parliament.

Henry Prust, the son of Robert, was in the English Navy and was engaged in the naval wars of the time. In **1337** he was master of King Edward III's ship *'La Trinite',* and he was present at King Edward the III's spectacular naval victory in **1340** at the battle of Sluys (shown here). This naval battle was part of the Hundred Years War (1337-1453) between England and France, which at a stroke, destroyed the French fleet, removed the threat of invasion, and secured English dominance for the time being. Henry Prust later gave up life at sea and went on to become a Member of Parliament for Torrington, sometimes referred to as Chipping Torrington in the county of Devon.

John Prust 'Canon of Windsor'
John Prust, son of Robert (mentioned on the previous page), entered holy orders and, in due course, was appointed one of the Canon of Windsor on May 26 **1379.** The College of Canons was established in 1348.
The Canon Stalls of the great Windsor Castle are shown here. John Prust retired in the year **1403**.

William Prust 'Yeoman of the Buttery'

This Yeoman' William Prust, was the second son of Richard Prust (the Richard born about **1280**). William was appointed by royal warrant patent to the position of *Yeoman of the Buttery* to King Edward III. A yeoman of the buttery oversaw the household food and drinks, including all the wine cellars. Additionally, he would have been in charge of all the staff connected with the day-to-day functioning of 'The Buttery.' The word 'Buttery' is derived from French and Latin words for bottle or, in the simpler form, a Butt, which is a cask. When King Edward III died in 1377, the young King Richard II came to the throne, and in 1378, confirmed the Royal favour to William Prust by granting him for life the custody of his wife Queen Phillipa's park and warren at a yearly allowance of one hundred shillings.

Thomas Prust, who was in service to the King. Thomas Prust, the second son of John, also served in the King's army, fighting in the One Hundred years' War. As a reward for his zeal, enthusiasm, and bravery, he was sent to the Abbot and Convent of Battle in Sussex, who were ordered to maintain him. Later in 1317, Thomas, feeling that he wanted to spend his days in the place he grew up in, was transferred to the Abbot and Convent of Monkleigh in Devon, where he continued to receive an allowance and keep.

Hugh Prust, the third son of John Prust, was also in the service of King Edward I (reigned from 1272 to 1307) and King Edward II (reigned from 1307 until deposed in 1327). It is not known in what capacity he served, but, after a long service to both kings, in 1329, he was sent to

the Abbott of Netele to receive such maintenance in their house at the king's request. Hugh was also mentioned as Bailiff to the Abbot at Ramsey in 1303 and 1304.
[Cat' of ancient deeds 21, Edward 1]

John Prust 'The Archer' There was also a John Prust who was born in about **1395** during the reign of) King Richard II (1377 to 1399). There is an online war record that there was an archer named John Prust who came from the village of Hartland in Devon. The law decreed at the time that young men from each village in England were ordered to practice archery on Sundays and on holidays; the local sheriffs enforced this law.

While bows have been used for hunting and warfare for thousands of years, few achieved the fame of the English Longbow. English archers were highly regarded and were expected to shoot ten "aimed" shots per minute during battle. A skilled archer would be capable of around twenty shots, as the typical archer was provided with 60-72 arrows to do this. Extensive training was required for medieval English longbowmen to become expert marksmen. The entire youth of the population was encouraged to take part in longbow sports so that at any given time, a large pool of expert English longbowmen was available to fight.

The aforementioned John Prust (recorded as John De La Preust dated 1432) was one of the archers chosen to fight in a battle of the one hundred Years' War when King Henry V decided to invade Normandy in France.). John Prust later fought at the siege of Harfleur, and his commander was the Duke of Exeter, Thomas Beaufort.

The archers were paid a wage of three pennies per day, and John was one of the sixty men in a garrison.

The Commander and military officer of the army was Sir Hugh Luttrell, a feudal baron and nobleman of Dunster in Somerset and close associate of his cousin King Richard II. Sir Hugh Luttrell was the son of Elizabeth Courtenay, great-granddaughter of Edward I of England. (I am mentioning this because in the early 17th century, some two hundred years later, another descendant of the Courtenay family 'Thomasine Courtenay' married into the Prust family of Devon

Note: the information above was taken from medieval military records of 1418 and the one hundred Years' War. (Now available online).

THE MIDDLE CLASSES IN MEDIEVAL ENGLAND

'In medieval England, there were three main aims for the middle classes. The first was to gain as much land as possible through influential marriages, especially female heiresses or as rewards for fighting for the King. The second was to marry for prestige and increase the circle of influential friends. And the third was to ensure that the pedigree line and lands stayed intact through male heirs.

When King William I conquered England, he divided all the lands amongst himself and his fellow supporters, many of them relatives. The only lands he did not own were the monastic lands owned by the church. These wealthy Barons then gave lands to other influential men in return for a knight's fee, which was the amount of money and/or military service a landowner was required to pay to support one knight. A person could provide the service of a knight or an equivalent amount of money to allow a lord to hire a knight.

These lands were usually passed on as an entailment unless they were given on life, in which case they would revert to the owner or the king on the person's death. Land was the keystone of social order, and it was essential to develop laws that ensured that the land would continue to be controlled indefinitely by those who owed their loyalty directly to the monarch. Medieval laws were therefore designed to deter disruption of land ownership patterns, including entailment, which placed conditions/limitations on succession to property by making it exceedingly difficult for the nobility to sell their land. Under entailment, a family, not an individual, owned land, and on the death of the current tenant, there would have been postmortem inquisitions, where all the lands were listed, and the next heir was named. This continued until the dissolution of the monasteries by Henry VIII, by which time the wealthy could buy these properties.

DESCENDANTS:

There are further direct descendants of this family in England and Wales and those early Prusts who migrated in the 19th century to start a new life in Australia, America, and Canada, who I will later connect to certain ancestors with a mark of an *asterisk.

There are also some descendants who migrated to Europe and South America, which have not been researched at the present time.

We will proceed with the line 'A' of the Visitation of 1620 with **Osbert Prust's descendants from the line of John.**

Going back to the beginning of the Visitation and some known facts about the following people. We will start with Osbert Prust and what is known about him.

Osbert was born in about **1150** and was the son of Richard Prust. He is named in a deed, and the date being given was **1199**. Unfortunately, the deed quoted by the Herald does not now appear to be in evidence. It may exist in some private collection and would throw more light as to what property the Prusts held and related to at this early date. Osbert was succeeded by his son and heir John Prust of Gorven, who was succeeded by his son and heir John Prust of Hartland, who was also called John Prest and distinguished himself in the King's foreign wars and for such good services is mentioned in the Patent Rolls. Then we have the missing at least three generation gap, which I have endeavoured to fill in; see page 40.

John Prust II was born during the reign of Henry IV (1399 to 1413) in the Visitation. In 1426 John Prust of Gorven by marrying **Agnes Holman**. She was the daughter and heiress of Thomas Holman, a gentleman (Re: Third paragraph of visitation) who was the Member of Parliament for the town of Barnstable in the county of Devon in about the year 1406. The Prust & Holman family coat of arms is shown here above.

The child of this marriage between John Prust IV and Agnes Holman appears to be an only son, also called John Prust of Hartland (V). The heralds say nothing further concerning him, nor do they give the name of his wife. John Prust had an issue: two sons.

1) **Peter Prust,** son and heir of John Prust, of whom hereafter (Re: page 48)

2) **John Prust** (Abbot Junior), The second son of John Prust of Hartland, quickly succeeded his cousin John Prust 'senior' in possession of the Abbots Chair; this was notified on August 18 **1529,** as Abbot of Hartland Abbey. See page 12, Re: Hartland Abbey.

HARTLAND MANOR HOUSE

We now know that at some time, John Prust resided at Hartland Manor House in the 16th century, as some of the Prust family was known to have lived there. Not to be confused with Hartland Abbey. Harland Manor house is still standing in Hartland today. However, it is now a hotel, as pictured here. Shown on the next page, there is an interesting newspaper article from 'The North Devon Journal Herald' dated July 4 **1950**, which records the find of a metal disc unearthed at Hartland Manor house, the home of the Prust family. The current owner at the time, Mr. Horace Prust, believed it to have belonged to Abbot John Prust.

Old Disc found at Hartland a Monk's Calendar?

A metal disc, believed to be gold, about the size of a half crown and containing numerous figures and lettering on each side, has been unearthed at Hartland Manor house during recent excavations. It is believed to be a monk's calendar, of the type carried by the monks and used for the purpose of the modern paper calendar. Mr. H. Prust, the owner of the Manor, believed the find may have had some connection with one of his ancestors, John Prust, who was a monk at the Abbey, but who was banished for four years to Lundy Island for breaking the rules. He afterwards returned to live at Hartland Manor. The Manor, which is mentioned in the Domesday Book, has some of its 'original walls standing, including a stone archway of Saxon origin in the main passage that contains the date 1084 cut roughly in the stone. It has always been in the Prust family, John Prust having come to England in the time of William the Conqueror. In the reign of Queen Elizabeth I some of the family continued the business as tanners, and some of the instruments used in the beating of the leather and bark are still retained at the

Manor. A few years ago, Mr. Prust found a silver piece embedded in one of the windows. It was thought to be a four-shilling piece.

Shown here is a close-up of one of the Manor House windows with dates etched on each side of **TGP 1706** and **TSP 1817**.

Hartland Money

Hartland Tannery in Hartland, Devon, is adjacent to Hartland Manor house, which was owned by the Prust family. In the 19th century, there was a shortage of small coinage in the country, so leather token money in values of sixpences and shillings was made in leather by Mr. Prust in the size and shape of a visiting card. This money was made to enable a trade to continue in the local area of Hartland at that time.

This picture above is not of the Prust leather coins but is similar to the ones that were around at the time.

Continuing: The Visitation from the Fifth Generation

Going down the fifth-generation line of the Visitation tree, we have

Peter Prust born about **1470,** son and heir of John Prust (IV), who succeeded his father at Hartland. He married; however, the name of his wife is unknown. He had one son **John Prust VI** who married **Isabel Drew,** daughter and co-heiress of John Drew Esquire. The Drew Coat of Arms is shown here together with the Prusts and Holmans. The Drews were a very ancient and influential Devon family, allied to the Courtenays and other well-known families from the area. The issue of this marriage was two sons and many daughters, namely:

Hugh Prust (1) **(1522 - 1581**). The son and heir of John Prust and **Isabel Drew**. He was known as **'Hugh Prust of Goven.'** Hugh succeeded his father in the parish of Hartland. There is a **(1)** document that Hugh Prust of Gorven was a tenant of three freehold farms in **1566** and was titled as a gentleman. Hugh played a prominent part in parish affairs in Hartland Hugh married twice, his first wife being **Alice Newcourt**

Here on the left is the Coat of Arms of the Newcourt family. Alice was the daughter of John Newcourt, Esquire, of Pickwell, in Devon. They had no children. Alice Prust was buried at Hartland on February 13 **1572**.

His second wife was **Agnes Wood,** who was born in **1535**. She was the daughter of Edmund or John Wood, Esquire of Orchard in Lew Trenchard, Devon. His son John Wood was a Member of Parliament for Bossiney in Cornwall in the year 1614. The Wood coat of arms is shown here, on the left. By this second marriage, Hugh Prust had seven children, four sons and three daughters. Hugh Prust died and was buried at Hartland in 1581.

Note: **(1)** Information regarding this document is from The Prust book of 1916.

2) **Lawrence Prust** was the second son of John Prust and **Isabel Drew**, he was of Tintagel, Cornwall, and he married **Joanna**

Quicke/Quyck on October 4 **1551**. Lawrence and Joanna Prust had three daughters and two sons. The first son, Richard Prust, was baptised in **1561,** and Lawrence Prust was baptised in **1566;** all his children were baptised in Knowstone, in the county of Devon. Lawrence Prust and Joanna, his wife, are named in the surrender at the Assession Court of the Manor of Tintagel, Cornwall, in **1579.** In the following years up to **1592** and beyond**,** Lawrence and Joanna Prust were in possession of the property known as Bossiney Park, otherwise known as 'Will Park' or Willapark, in the parish of Tintagel, in Cornwall. Bossiney Park was mentioned in the Doomsday Book and was the legendary stronghold of **King Arthur**. The borough of Bossiney was given the right to send two Members to Parliament in 1552 and continued to do so until 1832 when its status as a borough was abolished. It is almost certain that Lawrence and his wife Joanna

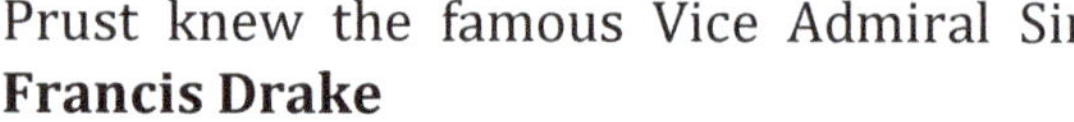

Prust knew the famous Vice Admiral Sir **Francis Drake**

Who is pictured here in the year 1582, as he held the parliamentary seat for the area of Bossiney, which was a parliamentary seat in Cornwall where he made many speeches? Sir Francis Drake was only a member of Parliament for one year until **1585.** Sir Francis Drake was famous for not only being a sea captain but a privateer and slaver; he was also a great favourite of Queen Elizabeth I of England. He died in the year 1596. Drake's second wife, Elizabeth, later married **Sir William Courtenay** of Powderham Castle in Exeter, Devon.

1) **Hugh Prust of Goven II (**Approximate birth date **1564)** died **in 1619**. The son and heir of Hugh Prust and Agnes Wood, his baptism does not appear in the parish register of Hartland, but his burial is given as June 23 **1619.** (More about him on page 56)

2) **Charles Prust** was born about **1569** at Gorven, Hartland Parish, in Devon. He was the second son of Hugh and Agnes Wood. Charles married **Honor Stone**. ('Stone' Coat of Arms pictured opposite) Honor was the daughter of John Stone, Esquire of Trevigo in Cornwall. Charles and Honor had five daughters: Temperance, Jane, Anna, Honor and Mary Prust.

They all married well, particularly Mary, who married John Escott, his coat of arms shown here. He was the Deputy to the Office of Arms for Devon and Cornwall and also was a direct descendant of King Henry I and King Stephen.

3) **James Prust**, third son of Hugh and Agnes Prust, married at Hartland to his cousin Alice Prust. She was the daughter of Lawrence and Joanne Prust. James died and was buried at Hartland on September 17 **1624.** They had one son **Charles Prust** who was baptised at Hartland on May 3 **1586.**

4) **Digory Prust** was the fourth son of Hugh and Agnes. In the year 1599, there was a Chancery proceeding in Devon between him, his wife Prudence, and two other named defendants. The plaintiffs were William Wythecombe, his wife Joan, and Philip Moulton. The plaintiffs were seeking to set aside deeds that they said were obtained by fraud. When Thomas Stearte, a gentleman, died, his daughter **Prudence Stearte** was said to be induced to sign a conveyance of her moiety of her father's lands, tenements, etcetera, before her marriage to William Wythecombe. The defendants were Phillip Moulton, Digory Pruste and Prudence, his wife & two others.
This above Information is from the 'Prust book of 1916, which also states: '*By the above suit we unearth the name and parentage of the lady, Digory Prust married, namely Prudence daughter and co-heiress of Thomas Stearte, gent'.*

There were various lands mentioned in this court case, including messuages, and one which I found of interest was in South Hole on the coast. The land of South Hole was previously owned by Robert Prust in about 1436. It was given to Robert Prust by his father, John Prust, who divided up his assets between his two sons, giving Robert 'South Hole and giving his other son John the land known as Goven in Hartland, which was said to be the most valuable.
(Source: Chancery proceedings temp Q, Elizabeth No.54. page 299)

The Prust Family and the Ship 'The Mayflower'

It is widely noted and supported by some historians that 'Digory Prust' or Priest, as it was sometimes spelt, was the son of Hugh and Agnes Prust of Harland in Devon, England. Digory (sometimes spelt Degory) was one of the original pilgrims on the famous ship 'The Mayflower,' which sailed from Plymouth, England, to America in 1620.

I can now take the opportunity to dispute this claim as upon looking through old documents that show Chancery Proceedings in 1599 in which he was involved and therefore gives the name of Digory's wife. It shows that Digory Prust, the fourth son of Hugh & Agnes Prust, was married to Prudence Steart, who lived and owned landed property in Devon, England. However, there is another person who was a possible link to 'The Mayflower,' as in this Prust family, I have unearthed another Digory Prust/Priest, which could well be him. There is a baptism record for a Digory Prust/Priest on August 11, **1582,** in Hartland, Devon. He was the son of Peter Prust and his wife, Wilmot Nichols. This Digory/Degory Priest/Prust had a brother John and a sister Agnes, and they all came from the county of Devon in England. The dates of his birth vary by different records, but it is known that he was deposed in 1619 in Leiden, Holland, in which he stated that he was 36 years old, so all dated point to the year 1582/3.

Digory Priest was part of the Leiden Contingent on the historic voyage of the ship 'The Mayflower' He was a 'Hatmaker' who owned property in London and was said to be born about 1579, so the dates could be about right. (Hat making was a good trade to have in England in those days, as everyone needed hats!) Digory married Sarah Allerton Vincent, a widow, and departed Plymouth in 1620. This man could well be the Digory Prust, who was one of 'The Pilgrim Fathers' on the *Mayflower* that went to America. Also on the voyage were Sarah Allerton's brother Isaac Allerton and his wife (who died in the first winter) and children who survived the voyage and settled in Plymouth. Isaac Allerton married three times and had many children. Many celebrities can claim that they are directly descended from the Mayflower pilgrims, including Clint Eastwood, Bing Crosby, Richard Gere, and Frankin D Rossevelt, the American president who is a descendant of Isaac Allerton.

Below is a copy of the compact that was signed on November 11, 1620. This document also became part of the American constitution.

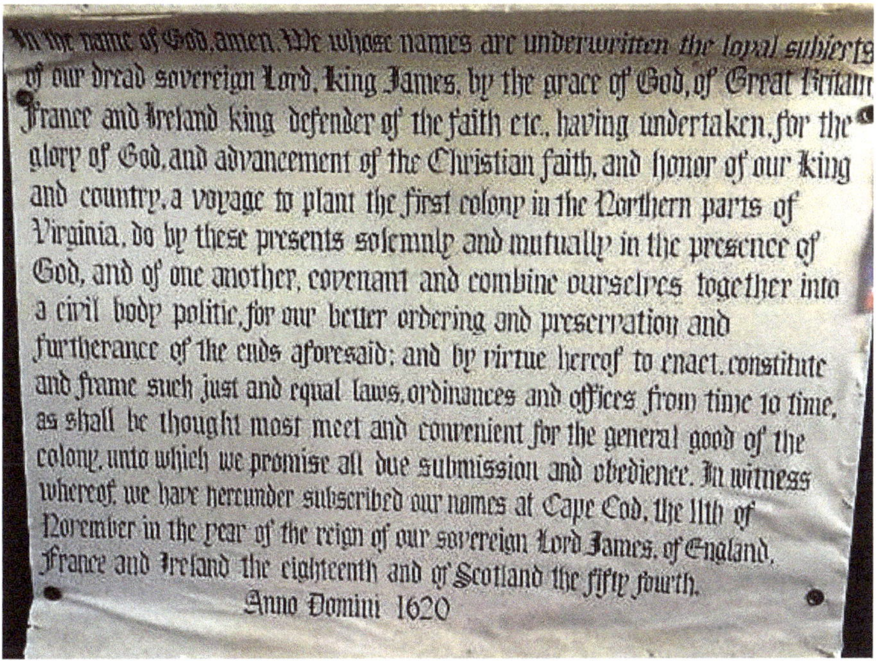

In the name of God, amen. We whose names are underwritten the loyal subjects of our dread sovereign Lord, King James, by the grace of God, of Great Britain France and Ireland king defender of the faith etc., having undertaken, for the glory of God, and advancement of the Christian faith, and honor of our King and country, a voyage to plant the first colony in the Northern parts of Virginia, do by these presents solemnly and mutually in the presence of God, and of one another, covenant and combine ourselves together into a civil body politic, for our better ordering and preservation and furtherance of the ends aforesaid; and by virtue hereof to enact, constitute and frame such just and equal laws, ordinances and offices from time to time, as shall be thought most meet and convenient for the general good of the colony, unto which we promise all due submission and obedience. In witness whereof, we have hereunder subscribed our names at Cape Cod, the 11th of November in the year of the reign of our sovereign Lord James, of England, France and Ireland the eighteenth and of Scotland the fifty fourth.

Anno Domini 1620

More about the Ship and its Captain

The ship 'The Mayflower was built in Harwich in Essex, which was a seafaring port in those days. Its captain was a man called Christopher Jones, and without him, this ship would not have made it across the Atlantic and with the fierce storms that brutalised them.

But who was Captain Christopher Jones and where did he come from, and how did he play such a vital role in the Mayflower story?

This is what I have found out about him as I live in Harwich myself. There are many references to him, as well as a museum set up on the pier with lots of information about not just the ship but the man himself:

Captain Jones was born in Harwich, Essex, and baptised in the local church of St Nicholas in about **1570** and was the son of Christopher Jones senior. He was also a Mariner and a ship owner himself.

Jones married Sara Twitt at St Nicholas Church in Harwich in December 1593 when she was 17. They were neighbours, living across the road from each other on Kings Head Street - both homes still exist and are now visitor attractions.

Sara's father, Thomas Twitt, was wealthy and had strong shipping interests. When he died, he left a 1/12 share in his ship Apollo and considerable money. Both Christopher and Sara's families combined their shipping interests. Within a year of the marriage, the couple had a son named Thomas, after her father, but records show he died in 1596. Sara had no more children and died at the age of 27 in 1603. Jones married his second wife, widow Josian Gray when she was 19. Josian had seafaring relatives, and her late husband, Richard Gray, was a noted mariner with friends among the captains of the 1588 Armada Fleet. Josian and Christopher's marriage produced eight children. Four of them were born in Harwich - Christopher, Thomas, Josian, and John. And four were born in Rotherhithe in London

It was in the year 1611 that Jones moved to Rotherhithe on the Southbank of the River Thames in London, and by this time, he had likely traded the ship *'Josian'* in for a quarter share in the Mayflower. Over the coming years, Jones worked in the wine trade, using the Mayflower to bring wine back from France, Spain, Portugal, and the Canaries, and in the summer of 1620, he and his ship were chartered to undertake the Pilgrim voyage across the Atlantic.

Captain Jones left Rotherhide In July 1620 and boarded the Mayflower with 65 passengers en route to Southampton to meet the ship Speedwell, bringing the Separatists from Leiden to Holland.

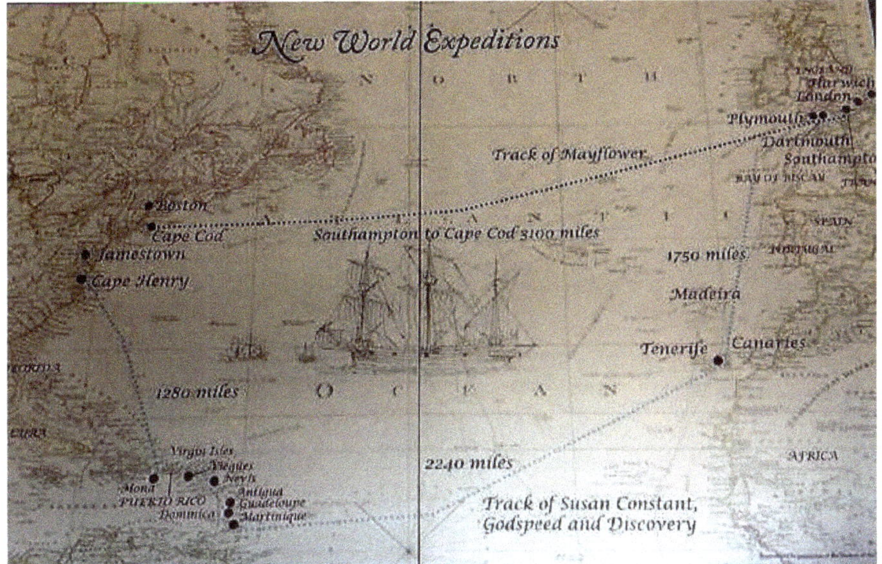

The journey continues: It was planned that both ships would sail across the Atlantic together, but bad weather and problems with Speedwell that could not be fixed meant the Mayflower was to sail alone with both ships' passengers. Some abandoned their journey and stayed in England, but the remaining 102 passengers left the Mayflower Steps in Plymouth on September 6, **1620,** and endured 66 days of fighting gales to cross the Atlantic, finally reaching the New World on November 11.

Jones and his ship remained in Plymouth Harbour, America, through the winter of 1620-1621, during which almost half the passengers died of a mixture of contagious diseases, which also hit some of Jones' crew.

At the start of April 1621, Jones and his crew left America and sailed back to England, arriving in their home port of Rotherhithe on May 5, 1621. He returned to his trading voyages, but his health had been badly affected by the trans-Atlantic journeys. He died in early March 1622 and was buried at St Mary's Church in Rotherhithe, where he lived.

The Mayflower ship was a 100-foot ship that had 102 passengers and a crew of about 20-30 men. The conditions were extremely cramped.

By the second month out, the ship was being buffeted by strong westerly gales, causing the ship's timbers to be badly shaken with caulking failing to keep out sea water and with passengers, even in their berths, lying wet and ill. This, combined with a lack of proper rations and unsanitary conditions for several months, contributed to illness that would be fatal for many, especially the majority of women and children. On the way, there were two deaths, a crew member and a passenger, but the worst was yet to come after arriving at their destination when, in the space of several months, almost half the passengers perished in cold, harsh, unfamiliar New England winter.

On November 9, 1620, after about three months at sea, including a month of delays in England, they spotted land, which was the Cape Cod Hook, now called Provincetown Harbour. After several days of trying to get south to their planned destination of the Colony of Virginia, strong winter seas forced them to return to the harbour at Cape Cod hook, where they anchored on November 11. The Mayflower Compact was signed that day.

Hugh Prust of Goven II

Hugh Prust's approximate birth date is **1564**, and he died in **1619** (Refer back to page 49). This Hugh was the son and heir of Hugh Prust & Agnes Wood. Hugh was an Overseer of the Peer in Hartland Church in 1604, and a document exists that he was the church treasurer in the year 1613. His position and status were given due recognition in the church when this pew was erected in the South Chapel of Hartland church in 1613. He had ordered the making of the pew, and the pew ends were carved with his initials 'HP'. The pew can still be seen today; see page 18. Like his father, Hugh married twice. His first wife was **Martha Anderton**; she was the daughter and co-heiress of John Anderton of Anderton in the parish of Launcells, Cornwall. With Martha, he had three sons***. Hugh's wife, Martha Prust, died and was buried at Hartland on July 3, **1588.**

Hugh Prust, in **1589,** married secondly to **Anne Carnsewe,** daughter of George Carnsewe, Esquire of Saint Kew in Cornwall. He and Anne had a large family of nine sons and two daughters. Shown here is a sketch of the Carnsewe coat of arms of a deer. Anne Prust outlived Hugh by fifteen years and was the executor of his will. When she died, she was buried at Hartland on the 7th of April, 1634. The children of Hugh Prust and Ann Carnsewe are on pages 58-60.

I will now give some history of the three sons of the first marriage of Hugh Prust and his wife, Martha Anderton. ***

1) **Hugh Prust of Monkleigh III** was baptised on 11 April **1584** and died in **1666**. He was the heir of Hugh Prust and Martha Anderton (more about him on page 60)

2) **Phillip Prust**, the second son of Hugh & Martha, was born about **1585**. He was of Emscott and Southhole in Hartland. Sources show that Philip was a churchwarden in the years **1618/9**. In **1634** there is a record where he refused to pay the 'Ship Money'. The ship money was a tax of medieval origin levied intermittently in the kingdom of England until the middle of the 17th century. Assessed typically on the inhabitants of coastal areas of England, it was one of

several taxes that English monarchs could levy by prerogative without the approval of Parliament! The attempt of King Charles I of England from 1634 onwards to levy ship money during peacetime and extend it to the inland counties of England without Parliamentary approval provoked fierce resistance and was one of the grievances of the English propertied class in the lead-up to the English Civil War. Phillip married twice, his first wife being **Mary Jewell,** who he married at Hartland on the 4 June **1615,** and by her, he had two children.

a) Henry Prust baptised at Hartland on 10 Feb **1621** and buried in 1621.

b) John Prust, baptised at Hartland on 1 Sept. **1626**. He married **Margery Clevedon** at Hartland on 28 Oct. **1652**. They had three daughters, Jane, Phillipa, & Mary Prust.

Philip Prust married, secondly, at Hartland on the 6 May **1633** to **Grace Bragge.** They had three children: John, Hugh & Thomasine Prust. Another line to explore!

3) **Robert Prust,** the third son of Hugh and Martha, died in infancy. He was baptised at Hartland on the 25 May **1588** and buried there on the 2 April **1589.**

Offspring of Hugh Prust of Goven II and Ann Carnsewe.

Hugh Prust of Goven II, by his second wife **Ann Carnsewe,** had eleven children.

4) Thomas Prust**,** fourth son of Hugh and first son of his second wife Ann, was baptised at Hartland on the 14 March **1590 or 1591.** He married on 2 June **1611** to **Mary Cooper,** by whom they had three sons and five daughters. No names are available at the present time.

5) Digory Prust, fifth son of Hugh and second son of Ann, was baptised at Hartland on the 4 June **1592** and buried there on 30 April **1600**, aged eight years old.

6) Henry Prust, sixth son of Hugh and third son of Ann. He was baptised at Hartland on the 15 Feb **1591**. He married **Mary Cary,** daughter of Thomas Cary, of Cary, Devon. In the Visitation of Devon of 1620, Henry was described as from Maryweeke in Cornwall.

7) Stephen Prust, seventh son of Hugh and fourth son of Ann. He was baptised at Hartland on 1 January **1593 or 1594** and was named in his father's will.

8) John Prust, the eighth son of Hugh and the fifth son of Ann, was also named in his father's will. He was born in about 1594.

9) Carnew Prust, the ninth son of Hugh and the sixth son of Ann, was obviously named in honour of her family name. He was baptised at Hartland on the 7 April **1595**, named in his father's will. He married at Hartland on the 30 January **1614** to **Anne Blagdon,** whose family crest is shown here; they had two children: Jane Prust in **1616** and John Prust in **1618**. Both were baptised at Hartland in Devon.

10) Richard Prust, the tenth son of Hugh and the seventh son of Ann, was baptised at Hartland on 1 July **1599**, named in his father's Will. He married **Ann Ackland,** daughter of Baldwin Ackland of Hawkridge, Devon.

11) Azarias Prust, the eleventh son of Hugh and the eighth son of Ann. He was baptised at Hartland on the 20 June **1603** and was named in his father's will. He married firstly (wife unknown) by whom he had an issue, one son and three daughters. More information as to the descendants is available on the internet at the genealogy site Ancestry. Mr. Azarias Prust (who is referred to as being of Southhole in Hartland) married secondly on 31 May 1646 to **Richarde Lang**. They had three children: John Prust, who was born and died in 1697, and two daughters, Susanna and Jane Prust.

12) Nicholas Prust, the twelfth son of Hugh and ninth son of Ann, was baptised at Hartland on 18 November **1604**. He married at Hartland to Miss **Christian Pawline**. They had one son Hugh Prust baptized in **1637.** He was buried at Hartland in **1684**.

13) Grace Prust, daughter of Hugh and Ann, was baptised at Hartland on 31 March **1602**. She married there on 10 April 1624 to **John Vine**.

14) Radagon Prust, daughter of Hugh and Ann, was baptised at Hartland on 12 December **1600**. She married **Arthur Holman** on 30 September 1618. And lastly, 15) Martha Prust, daughter of Hugh & Ann, born about **1601.**

Hugh Prust of Monkleigh 1584–1666

Prust Coat of Arms Carey Coat of Arms

Hugh Prust III of Goven Esquire **(**from page 63), also known as Hugh Prust of Monkleigh, was the eldest son and heir of Hugh Prust of Goven in Hartland and his first wife Martha, daughter, and co-heiress of John Anderton of Anderton, in Cornwall. His baptism does not appear in the parish register, being born and baptised elsewhere. He was an Attorney of Law, and he was named in his father's will in 1619 and in that of his eldest son Hugh who died during his lifetime in **1650.** He succeeded his father at Goven but appeared to have settled at Monkleigh in Devon, where he was buried on 1 May **1666.** Like his father and grandfather, Hugh married twice. His first wife was Anne Carey, daughter of Francis Cary, Esquire, of Clovelly, in Devon. Anne Carey was baptised at Alwington Devon in **1587 or 1588**, and she and Hugh had nine children, as detailed forthwith. This amazing portrait, shown on the next page, was found in London by Ann, painted after her death in 1628.

Ann Carey, the Wife of Hugh Prust

This is a Memento Mori portrait of Anne Prust, which was painted sometime after her death in 1628. She died, according to the writing on the painting, on the 12th of February 1628, aged 40 years old. This was shortly after giving birth to her tenth child, a daughter named Susan. The portrait is painted in oil on board. Ann is attired in typical early 17th-century period clothing. One hand is shown touching a skull, which signifies that the sitter of the painting has died. The background on the left shows the coats of arms of the Prust and Carey families. The text in the portrait is in Latin and says, '*Memento Mori'*, which means 'Remember that you have to die'. The painting was on sale at Sotheby's, a well-known auction house in London, England. It was sold as an 'Old Master' and described incorrectly as a portrait of Hugh Prust for an estimate of 4000 to 6000 pounds in 2017.

Hugh Prust and Elizabeth Coffin/Coffyn

Eight months after Ann died, Hugh Prust married again, and on 27 October 1628, at Alwington, Devon, he married **Elizabeth Coffin**, nee Hardinge, daughter of Henry Hardinge Esquire, and widow of John Coffin Esquire., of Porthledge Manor, shown here is the House belonging to the Coffin family. This house sits on the edge of Bideford Bay, looking out over the Bristol Channel in the parish of Alwington and the surrounding area and was given to the family by William the Conqueror as part of a reward for loyalty and service during the Norman Conquest. With this marriage also came great wealth for the Prust family.

John Coffin died in 1622, aged only 30 years old, leaving Elizabeth with four children. The Coffin family and the Prust family were well known to each other as the Coffin family also had property in Monkleigh, where the Prust family resided. In fact, the eldest daughter of John and Elizabeth Coffin, Jane Coffin, later went on to marry **Hugh Southy Prust Jnr., 1614-1650**, the son of Hugh Prust of Goven (1584-1666). Sadly, Jane Coffin died a year later, and they had no children. The other children of John and Elizabeth Coffin and stepchildren to Hugh Prust were Gertrude Coffin 1621-. Richard Coffin 1622-1699 and Elizabeth Coffin 1623-1653. Interestingly in **1665,** Hugh Prust (1584-1666), just one year before his death, transferred Goven lands to his stepson Richard Coffin Esquire who was then the High Sheriff of Devon.

Shown here is an oil portrait of Richard Coffin Esquire, which gives an insight into the attire of a 17th-century gentleman. This painting was later sold by a well-known auction house for an undisclosed sum of money.

Hugh Prust, already the father of nine children by his first wife Ann Carey, went on to have a further two children with his second wife Elizabeth Coffin; they were **Emme Prust** 1634-1700, who married **Richard Yeo** of Bradworthy, Devon and **Rebecca Prust** 1637. Elizabeth Prust died and was buried at Alwington on the 9th of October, **1668.**

Hugh Prust of Monkleigh, who had the title of *Gentleman,* was also an Attorney and Solicitor of law. One record of particular interest is the case of *Prust v Pincombe* (which can be found in the National Archives).

This case was against a fellow lawyer, which was interesting and could be amusing to us in the 21st century! This is about Hugh Prust of Monkleigh, in Devon, who brought proceedings against a Barrister of the Middle Temple in the Court of Chivalry. The Court of Chivalry is a court that hears matters relating to heraldry. On the following page is a summary of the case.

Prust V Pincombe

On the 17th of April **1640,** a case was brought before the Court of Chivalry at the Exeter Assizes held at Exeter Castle.

Mr. Prust and Mr. Pincombe were two men in their late fifties; they were having supper together at the Black Swan Inn in the company of other gentlemen when an argument broke out between these two elderly men. Whereupon Mr. Prust, an attorney at law, complained that Pincombe, a barrister of the Middle Temple, had said to him (written in the language of the 17th century), *"Thou art a wicked fellow, an ungodly fellow. Thou canst not go to heaven, thou must go to hell. I am a better man than thou art and better descended by both mother and father".*

A witness for Mr. Pincombe said he was present at the argument, but he could not remember the words that passed between them. Another witness stated that he had known Pincombe for 20 years, and during that time, he lived as a gentleman and was termed esquire; he verily believed that Mr Prust was inferior in gentry unto Mr Pincombe. He had heard that Prust was a man of turbulent disposition and troublesome to his neighbours and so commonly reputed. He had heard Pincombe held the degree of an utter barrister, and when he hath been disposed of (Drunk, maybe?) He caused a drum to be beaten, and at which sound, the poor people flocked about him to whom he hath literally bestowed money unto. Apparently, the two men quarrelled over a debt owed by Pincombe to Prust, which resulted in Prust bringing lawsuits in Castle Court and the Stannary Court. There was also a countersuit to Pincombe's case against Prust in the Court of Chivalry, which was underway. According to witnesses, Prust had endeavoured to smear Pincombe's reputation by claiming that he '*beat up his drum late at night, to lead his guard of soldiers from alehouse to alehouse'*; but he explained that when Pincombe was merrily disposed of, he had a habit of beating the drum to summon up the untrained band and would then disburse money to the local paupers.

This was a case when both sides could claim some sort of victory.

Prust was required to perform a submission to Pincombe on his suit, but in this instance, on 3 September 1640, Pincombe was ordered to pay Prust £90 in costs and damages and perform a submission before the judge of the Assizes at Exeter Castle in which he was required to apologize and acknowledge Prust's gentility and promise to behave *'with due respect towards Mr. Prust and all gentry of this kingdom'.* Pincombe was to perform his submission 'standing bareheaded' before the judge of the assizes, stating that I, John Pincombe, stand convicted to have used divers provoking speeches to and against Hugh Prust of Monkleigh Devon gent and to have used the following words *Prust "Thou art a wicked fellow, an ungodly fellow. Thou canst not go to heaven, thou must go to hell. I am a better man than thou art and better descended by both mother and father."* I do now Hereby confess and acknowledge that Hugh Prust is a gent descended from an ancient family bearing arms and that I did him much wrong by uttering provoking speeches and am heartily sorry for the same. And I do promise for the future not to offend in the like kind but to carry myself with due respect towards Mr. Prust and all gentry of this kingdom.

This concluded the case of both men who claimed a victory, but who do you think is the winner!
Hugh Prust, who died in 1666, outlived his son and heir Hugh Prust, 1614-1650, by sixteen years.

The children of Mr. Hugh Prust by his first wife, Ann Carey, are as follows:
1) Hugh Prust of Monkleigh (II) 1614-1650, son and heir of Hugh Prust and Anne Carey, his wife. Hugh was also known as Hugh Southy Prust. He was baptised on 27 February **1614** at Bideford, in Devon. He married at Monkleigh on 19 May **1645** to **Jane Coffin,** eldest daughter of John Coffin Esquire, and she was also his stepsister as his father Hugh married Mrs. Elizabeth Coffin, as previously stated on page 62.

The Prust family were mostly all Royalists, and in particular, Hugh Prust was known to be a staunch Royalist. He fought bravely against the Parliamentarians in The English Civil War. Shown above here is a picture of 'The Battle of Naseby' at which the Royalists lost against the Parliamentary roundheads. It was the year 1643, and near the start of the English Civil War, Parliament had set up two committees, one, the Sequestration Committee, which confiscated the estates of the Royalists who fought against Parliament, and the 'Committee for Compounding with Delinquents' which allowed the Royalists whose estates had been sequestered (confiscated the property) to compound for their estates, pay a fine and recover their estates if they pledged not to take up arms against Parliament again. The size of the fine they had to pay depended on the worth of the estate and how great their support for the Royalist cause had been. Sadly, Hugh Prust of Monkleigh in Devon had his large estates confiscated by Parliament.

This is a quote from 'The Committee of Compounding' dated 6 April 1648 *'In list of papists and delinquents sequestered in north Devon since the happy reduction of the county to the obedience of Parliament in 1646* was *the name of 'Hugh Prust of Monkleigh delinquent and notorious' (committee for compounding*)'.
After the restoration of the monarchy in 1660, most of the sequestrated land was returned to the pre-war owners, but not always!

Hugh's will is dated August 1650, only one month before he died. It has two codicils and was proved in the following year, 1651. Hugh died only aged 36 years old. He had an illness and knew that death was imminent and died during his father's lifetime. He was buried at Monkleigh, in Devon, in September **1650**. His wife Jane Prust died four years previously, only one year after their marriage and was also buried at Monkleigh. In the church at Monkleigh, there is a monument with an inscription to their memory. As Hugh and his wife Jane had no children, all his assets went to his brother Joseph Prust of Annery in Devon.
This substantial house below was owned by the Prust family, most first by Hugh and then passed on to his son Joseph.

Annery House, Monkleigh, Devon

The first family member who can with certainty be identified as living at Annery is Lieutenant Colonel Joseph I Prust, who was baptised in **1620** at Bideford in Devon.

Joseph Prust of Annery 1620-1677 was the second son of Hugh Prust and his first wife, Ann Carey. Joseph and his brother Hugh were named as a beneficiary in his brother Hugh's will. Joseph was also a staunch Royalist like his brother and fought in the English Civil War. Joseph held the rank of Lieutenant Colonel in the regiment of Horse of Sir Thomas Stuckley of Affeton Castle. At the siege of Plymouth in **1642-1646, It is recorded that Lieutenant Colonel Joseph Prust had the misfortune to lose a hand in that battle**.

Joseph married at Hartland on 2 March **1651** to Anne Keynes, daughter and co-heiress of John Keynes Esquire. Ann Prust died aged just thirty years old, leaving two small sons, and was buried at Monkleigh in Devon in March **1659**, and in the church in Hartland, there is an inscription to her memory.

Fast forward some seven years later, and it is found that on the 25th of March **1653**, a deposition by Jeffrey Sampson of Clement Danes in the county of Middlesex that 33-year-old Joseph Prust was a Captain of the foot company in Exeter Castle and Lieutenant Colonel of horse in Colonel Stuckley's regiment. He was commanded abroad on other services ten weeks before Exeter Castle surrendered to Lord Capel, and two months after the surrender, he (Prust) repaired to Goldsmiths Hall and took an oath that he was not worth £200 and consequently was discharged from the composition according to the ordinance of parliament in that behalf. I cannot see this being true unless his house was confiscated, which might have been the case as he fought against the government at that time.
(*Source: The National Archives: The Committee for compounding P.3100*).
Lieutenant Colonel Joseph Prust died aged 57 years old and was buried at Monkleigh on the 17th of October **1677**. There is a ledger stone in memory of Joseph Prust of Annery in Annery Chapel, Monkleigh Church, Monkleigh, in Devon. The stone has the 'Prust' coat of arms sculpted in relief and is engraved with these words:

"Here lieth interred Joseph Prust of Annerie gent. sometime leiutent colon'l of horse to sr. Thomas Stuckley in his Maj'ties service of blessed memory Charles the First in which he lost one of his hands in fight before Plimouth.
(It goes on to inscribe the following poem in the language of that time!)

How law, religion, loyalty did fall,
How first we lost the king and church then all,
Experience shews 'twas because few at need
Who much pr'tended proud th'r freinds indeed,
Here's one stood firme and gave his hand to own,
Wr to but name at length was treason grown,
Rebellions like the Hydra's heads doe grow,
One cut of here and two rise up below,
His hand such monsters knew how to suppress,
Briareus hundred hands can't soe redress,
Oh Heaven's grant we nere may see again,
The raging dogstaro'retop Charles his wain,
Nor yet the wolfe usurp the lion's crown,
Rebellion rampant and allegiance down,
But if the fates such times should have decreed,
How much such hands as his was shall we need".

His will was proved in the Principal Registry at Exeter in **1677**. Joseph and Ann had four children:

1) Prust, born **1656-1656,** died in infancy.

2) Joseph Prust II, **1658-1692,** died without issue.

3) Anne Prust was baptised at Monkleigh on 29 December **1659**,

4) Captain John Prust **1660-1695.** It is known that John Prust was born at Monkleigh in Devon on the 6 Feb 1660. He was heir to his father's estates, and he was a Captain in the Army. Captain John Prust married **Mary Leigh,** daughter of Thomas Leigh Esquire, at Monkleigh on 2 April **1690**. The Leigh family Crest is shown here. John Prust died in 1695, aged just 35 years old and was buried at Monkleigh in Devon. John and Mary had three sons and one daughter.

Sadly, all three sons died in infancy, so their only daughter Ann was the sole heir.

ANN PRUST and RICHARD ANNESLEY, The 6TH EARL of ANGLESEY.

Ann was born and baptised in **1694**. She was the daughter of John Prust and Mary Leigh. A marriage was arranged between the rich heiress Ann Prust and the titled Richard 6th Earl of Anglesey, Baron Altham of Ireland, and many other titles, including my title of a 'scoundrel' a blaggard and a bigamist and his contemporaries at the time, called him "a most terrible of human beings" and "The greatest rogue in Europe."

The wedding of Ann Prust and Richard Earl of Anglesey took place on 24 January **1715**, when she was just 19 years old. Ann Prust was a rich heiress and brought him a considerable fortune. From family records, it is known that Richard deserted her almost immediately after their marriage, as in the same year of 1715, Richard went over to Ireland to see to his estates and land, and there he met and bigamously married a 15-year-old girl called Ann Simpson, the daughter of a wealthy clothier in Dublin. Richard and Ann Simpson had three daughters. Although Richard was a charmer of women, he had a dark and evil character, as evidence shows.

Ann Simpson believed she was legally married and had no knowledge of another wife in England. In about 1740, Richard repudiated his marriage, declared his children illegitimate and turned them all out of his house. Ann Simpson claimed she was forced to quit the house of Richard Annesley due to his cruelty. In **1741** Ann Simpson took proceedings against Richard in the ecclesiastical court on the grounds of cruelty and adultery, with a view of obtaining permanent alimony. He set up by way of defence that he was lawfully married to Ann Prust at the time when he was alleged to have gone through the ceremony with Ann Simpson, and the lady appears to have gained nothing by her suit, although an interim order was made for £4 per week, payment was never made, and they all suffered great distress and hardship.

There is a record of a remarkable document signed by her ladyship Ann Prust of Annesley in 1726 wherein she binds herself (promised) never to prosecute her husband for bigamy, which certainly looks like both parties considered the marriage with Ann Prust to be legal. Lady Ann of Annesley died without issue and was buried at Monkleigh in **1748.** Upon hearing of his first wife's death, Richard Earl Annesley returned to Ireland and married again. In **1752** he married another young heiress, seventeen-year-old Juliana Donovan, whose mother possessed considerable estates in Ireland. By this lady, Richard had four children, including a son Arthur. In **1761** Richard became gravely ill, and upon hearing of her father's illness, Dorothea, the eldest daughter of Ann Simpson, undertook the journey to Camolin Park in Wexford to induce him to acknowledge his marriage to her mother. She heard that her father had made a will leaving her only five shillings in quit of all demands as his natural daughter. Dorothea was repulsed with much indignity by the women then claiming to be the Earl's wife. By this time, Dorothea was a mother herself, having married a French musician and became the famous Dorothea Du Bois, Irish poet, Autobiographer, and musical dramatist in her own right. Ann Simpson survived the Earl dying in 1765, leaving three daughters, Dorothea, Caroline, and Elizabeth.

Richard died in **1761**, In county Wexford, Ireland, and upon his death, two petitions were presented to the Earl of Halifax, the lord lieutenant of Ireland: One by Sir John Annesley and the other by Countess Juliana on behalf of her son Arthur. During the progress of this inquiry, the issue came to depend on whether a certain marriage certificate bearing the date **1741** was genuine or not. The countess swore that she secretly married the late earl in 1741 and produced a certificate in evidence. On the other hand, a witness swore that the certificate had been made out at the date of the marriage in 1752 and purposely altered. As the witnesses to the alleged marriage were all dead, the case for Countess Juliana broke down, but countess Juliana took her claim on behalf of her infant son Arthur to the Earl of Halifax. The committee determined that Arthur's claim was successful, and he accordingly, on coming of age, took his seat in the Irish House of Lords. However, he was not so successful in the proceedings he took to make good his claim to the English Earldom, as it was decided that he had no right to that title nor the honours and dignities claimed by him. His claim to the English peerage accordingly became extinct. In the will of

Richard Earl of Anglesey, we unearth his nine surviving children by four different women. His children by his present wife, Countess Juliana, were Lady Richearda, Lady Juliana, Lady Catherine, and Arthur Annesley, otherwise known as Lord Annesley. He also stated in his will that whilst being separated from his wife, Ann Prust, afterwards Countess of Anglesey, he had children by the following women. By Mrs. Ann Simpson, he had the following three daughters, Dorothea Annesley, Carolina Annesley, and Elizabeth Annesley. By Mrs. Ann Saulkeld of London, he had a son Richard Annesley, and by Mrs. Mary Glover, he had a daughter, Ann Annesley.

The Story of a Kidnapping

This is a true story about a sensational trial of the 18th century regarding Richard Annesley, the husband of our Ann Prust. This case was brought against Richard Annesley, the sixth Earl of Anglesey, by his nephew James Annesley in **1743.**

James Annesley's allegation was that in the year **1727,** he became heir to the Earldom when his father died. The young James said his uncle had him kidnapped and shipped to America as an indentured servant and thereby stole his title! Undoubtedly Richard Annesley was a rotter; he married bigamously, lied, cheated, bullied, and in a tawdry, beggarly fashion, scandalised the tolerant morals of his fellow peers. He borrowed money that was not repaid, cut down valuable timber on estates that he didn't own, and left bastards unprovided for. Nevertheless, aristocrats were part of the government and not easily displaced. When the Earl took to calling young James 'The pretender', it associated his claim with that of his peers with that of Scotland's 'Charles Stuart' who claimed to be the rightful king. So, the implications were obvious to a 1740 audience; if one pretender was allowed to take the earl's coronet, then why shouldn't another take King George II's crown?

At the trial, however, a trail of evidence revealed the full extent of the villainous earl's campaign against his nephew.

It all began when he hired two ruffians to bundle the 12-year-old boy onto a ship bound for America and bribed the captain to present him in the colonies as a ten-year-old indentured servant (being small for his age), effectively making him a slave for that time.

James later told of his traumas escaping and being recaptured twice eventually. The third time, he escaped on a boat going to Jamaica, and when he explained his plight to the captain, who went ahead and checked his story. So, at last, he was returned to England. Nevertheless, when the young man at last returned, his barely credible story was immediately believed.

At the trial, the earl was getting alarmed and was just about to decide to negotiate a compromise when an extraordinary accident handed him a trump card as follows: Richard, upon hearing a story that while out shooting James killed a poacher, he decided to act. So, on Richard Anglesey's instructions, his lawyer bribed a witness to say that the young man had levelled the gun at the victim deliberately.

James was then charged with MURDER and was liable to be hanged. But by another switch of fortune, a surgeon took the trouble to probe the wounds, and the trajectory confirmed James's testimony that the gun went off accidentally as he carried it low to the ground. Set free, James went to Ireland, where he was immediately acclaimed as the rightful heir. In final desperation, the psychopathic Earl invited James to the races in Curragh, where he arranged not one but two attempts at assassination.

This tale twists further before the end as, after an appeal, James fails to establish his claim in England, and the Earl continues to be Earl until his death in 1761.

It has been speculated that the novel 'KIDNAPPED' (the front cover of the novel is shown here) was inspired by this true story from earlier in the 18th century. It is also inconceivable that Robert Louis Stephenson, the author of the book, was not aware of this famous court case which was widely published at the time. And that had similarities to our true story.

I will now return to the other children of Hugh Prust and Anne Carey: (refer back to pages 64 & 65, where I have mentioned the first and second child).

3) **Abraham Prust,** born in **1622.** The third son of Hugh and Anne. He was named in the will of his brother Hugh in 1650. He is also named in the records of Oxford University Alumni, attending Exeter College, which records him as "Son of Hugh of Monkleigh, Gent. 8 March 1638/40 aged 16 years".

4) **John Prust**, the fourth son of Hugh and Anne, was also named in the will of his brother Hugh in 1650. A small excerpt from his brother's will say this: *thus "Unto my three brothers Joseph, Abraham & John Prust the sum of five pounds apiece."*

John Prust was, in all probability, baptised at Woolfardisworthy in Devon and married in **1644** to **Agnes Pawline**. When she died, she was buried at Hartland in the year **1673**. John and Agnes had two children, and I have detailed them further down this page as this branch of the family goes forward to the present time **

Hugh and Ann had further five daughters and one son.

5) **Elizabeth Prust**, daughter of Hugh & Anne, she was baptised on the 13 March **1612** at Bideford. She married at Monkleigh to **John Elston**, and they were both living in 1650.

6) **Mary Prust**, daughter of Hugh & Anne, she was baptised on the 26 December **1615** at Bideford and married in the village of Alwington, Torridge, Devon on the 29 October 1656 to **John Vigurs**.

7) **Frances Prust,** daughter of Hugh & Anne, baptised on the 1 February **1617** at Bideford and was living unmarried in 1650.

8) **Julian Prust**, son of Hugh & Anne, baptised. 10 October **1624** at Hartland, and buried at Monkleigh 14 October **1688, a**ged 64 years.

9) **Martha Prust,** born about **1627,** and lastly, 10**) Susan Prust,** born **1628.**

Prust Families of Hartland in the 17th-18th Century

****The family of John Prust and Agnes Pawline**
(Information from: 'The Prust Book' of 1912)

a) **John Prust,** son of John Prust and Agnes Pawline, his wife, was baptised at Hartland in **1645**. John married **Elizabeth Lendon** in Hartland on 6 May 1678. And with her, he had five children. Elizabeth Prust (1677-1711), Joseph Prust (1678-1729), Anne Prust (1680-1765), Grace Prust (1687-), and Thomas Prust (1690-1778).

b) **Joseph Prust**, the second son of John & Agnes, was also born at Hartland in **1646**. His will is dated 18 June **1714**, in which he is described as "of Hartland" Devon, Yeoman. Joseph Prust married **Grace Galsworthy** on 26 October **1676**. Grace was buried at Hartland on 28 January **1724**.
The following abstract is of Joseph's will:

'He gives to his dear wife one estate called Boscombe in the parish of Parkham and also messuages, lands, & tenements in the parish of Hartland for life, and after his decease to his heir & executer named. Gives wife certain household goods and all her gold rings etc., during her life, and after her decease bequeaths same to his daughter Grace Prust. Gives to daughter Grace Prust £20 two years after she attains full age of 21. Gives to son Thomas Prust £5 and a bed. Gives to granddaughter Mary Mugford £10 and a tableboard now in her father's house. Gives grandson William Prust 5/- when of full age.
Gives residue of his estate to his son John Prust and makes him executor. Appoints friends 'John Lee & John Mugford of Hartland to be executors in trust. Witnesses: - John Foster, Thomas Rowe & Richard Davie'
Mr. Joseph Prust must have been on his deathbed when he made his will, as he was buried at Hartland on 22 June **1714**, four days after the making of his will.

Joseph Prust and Grace Galsworthy had six children, four sons and two daughters:
1) **William Prust**, the first son of Joseph & Grace, he was baptised at Hartland on 19 February **1679**.

2) **Joseph Prust,** second son of Joseph & Grace, was baptised at Hartland on 7 Sep**t. 1682** and buried at Hartland on 5 Dec **1729**. He married **Mary Littlejohns** on 14 February 1710 at Hartland, and they had a son William Prust *(**1713-1789),** and a daughter Judith Prust (**1720-1759).**

William Prust, *(**1713**) was named in his grandfathers will. He was baptised at Hartland on 24 April **1713** and married **Elizabeth Vine** on 7 June **1736**, and she was the daughter of Mr. Michael Vine. William Prust died and was buried at Hartland on the 3 Oct **1789**. He is described as 'a tanner of Hartland' in the parish of Hartland. The following is an abstract of his will:

Gives son William £1.1.0d (one guinea) (One year after his death. Gives son Michael £1.1s.0d They giving executor receipt Gives son Joseph £1.1s.0d in full of all demands) Gives daughter Sarah £140, one year after his decease, provided she conveyed and assigned to executor all her share of testator's real estate, which she would be entitled to, as by testator's marriage settlement. Gives daughter Margaret £50 one year after his decease, and a further sum of £70, two years after decease, on the proviso as above.
Joseph, William & Elizabeth, sons, and daughter of testator's son William £1 each, and unto Elizabeth wife of said son William £1.1.0.
Gives residue of estate to son Thomas Prust, his executor etc., and appoints him sole executor and residuary legatee.
Gives said son Thomas his heirs and assigns all real estate lands, tenements and hereditaments situate in Harton in Harland & elsewhere for ever:
This Will was proved at Bideford on the 27 April **1790**.

William Prust (1713) & Elizabeth Vine had eight children.

1) William Prust, baptised at Harland on the 6 March **1736,** and he married there on the 5 Nov **1769** to **Elizabeth Rowe** of Downe in North Hartland, Devon. Their five children were:

a) Joseph Prust, baptised on 11 Oct **1770**, he married **Mary Hooper,** and they had five children. Joseph Prust died in 1830, leaving a son Joseph Hooper Prust. Who was last recorded as being at the British Naval Base of Simon's Bay, Cape Colony, South Africa, in **1846**? And nothing was heard from him since.

b) William Prust, baptised on the 13th Feb **1775**

c) Elizabeth Rowe Prust (**1772 -1854)**

d) Catherine Prust, baptised on 19 May **1776**

e) Ann Prust, baptised on 4 Dec. **1777**.

2) Joseph Prust, the second son of William Prust and Elizabeth Vine born and died in **1738**.

3) **Reverend Michael Prust**, third son of William Prust and **Elizabeth Vine,** was baptised on 19 March **1741** and matriculated from Exeter College, Oxford, on 14 March 1761. B.A.

4) Thomas Prust, born in **1744** and buried at Hartland in **1745.**

5) Joseph Prust, baptised in **1746** and buried at Hartland in **1751.**

6) Thomas Prust, baptised, and was buried in Hartland in **1751.**

7) Reverend Joseph Prust, baptised at Hartland on the 16 March **1755**. Matriculated at Magdalen Hall, Oxford on the 2 March **1774**. He was afterwards of Wembworthy, Devon. The Rev. Joseph Prust married in 1774 to **Mary Budd**. They had two children.

a) **Daniel Prust,** born in **1775** and died at sea aged 22 yrs.

b) **Thomas Prust,** born in **1779,** married **Jane Balhatchet**. **

8) Thomas Prust, the eighth child and son of William Prust and Elizabeth Vine. He was baptised at Hartland on the 5 May **1751** and buried there on the 12 December **1829,** aged 72 yrs. He married by license at Hartland on 12 March **1794** to **Sarah Ching**, daughter of Mr. Thomas and Mrs. Elizabeth Ching. They had 12 children. Mrs. Sarah Prust was buried on 11 March **1864**.

9) Anne Prust, the ninth child and daughter of William Prust and Elizabeth, she was baptised at Hartland on the 30 January **1739** and buried in **1746**, aged seven years old.

10) Sarah Prust, the tenth child and daughter of William Prust and Elizabeth, she was baptised on 17 February **1748** at Hartland. She later resided at Bideford in Devon.

11) Margaret Prust, the eleventh child of William Prust and Elizabeth, was baptised on 15 January **1753**. She later lived at St. Cubert in Cornwall.

The children of Thomas Prust **(No. 8)** and his wife, Sarah Ching, were:

a) **William Prust** baptised on 26 June **1791** (William was three years old before his parents' marriage) and went by both names of Ching and Prust. He married on the 7 May 1828 to **Sarah Ellis,** daughter of Mr. Henry Ellis, and Sarah Heard, his wife. They had two sons, twins, namely Richard and Edward Prust.

b) **Michael Prust,** baptised on 3 November. **1794.**

c) **Joseph Prust**, baptised on 30 June **1796**

d) **Thomas Prust,** baptised and buried in November **1797.**

e) **Thomas** Prust, born and died in **1799**.

f) **Sarah Ann Prust,** baptised at Hartland on 16 June **1800** and died **in 1883. S**he remained unmarried. She left in her will money to her nephew Richard Prust, the son of her brother William Prust.

g) **Margaret Elizabeth Prust,** baptised at Hartland on 23 August 1801, married **James Lendon** and had an issue.

h) **Betty Prust,** baptised at Hartland on 15 August **1802**; Betty married **Richard Stone** of Hartland.

i) **Thomas Prust**, born **1804** and died at Hartland in **1805**,

j) **Daniel Prust** ** baptised at Hartland on 20 March **1808** and married there on 22 May 1830 to **Grace Foot Rowe**. (More about Daniel and Grace on page: 82).

k) **Thomas Prust**, born in April **1806 -1891.** Thomas and his wife Sarah were insistent on having a son called 'Thomas' as he was the fourth one they named and survived into adulthood. More is known about **Thomas Prust** (Born 1806) through the court proceedings against him for bigamy. Thomas married twice, his first wife was **Mary Pillman,** who he married in **1828**, and then he married again bigamously to **Eliza Stone** in **1839,** eleven years later. Thomas was charged with the crime of bigamy in **1841**.

A slightly shorter transcript of the charges against him is as follows, which were taken from the Western Times newspaper. This interesting case brings the reader back to the thought and the language of 19th-century England. I have given below an excerpt of this fascinating court case.

Thomas Prust - A Case of Bigamy

From: The Western Times March 1841

Mr R Smith prosecuted, and Mr Cockburn defended the prisoner. Mr Smith briefly stated the case. The prisoner stood charged with having intermarried with Eliza Stone on the 21st of March 1839, his former wife, Mary Pillman, who he had married on the 17th of April 1828, being still living, and he is having knowledge that she was so living within seven years of his contracting the second marriage.

Mr J Pillman was the first witness called. He said - I am a farmer residing at Hartland, in this county; was present at the marriage of my sister Mary at Hartland Church; on the 17th of April 1828 Thomas Prust, the prisoner, is the person who married Mary Pillman; after their marriage, and subsequently at Bideford; in 1832

Cross-examination continued - My sister sailed for America in March 1832; she occasionally wrote to my father and mother; the prisoner about that time resided at Bideford; several months before his marriage, I heard that he was likely to be married again.

You sent for her after the prisoner's second marriage? No, I did not.

Did any of your family? Not that I know of.

Who pays the expenses of this prosecution? I do not,

But some others of the family? They may do.

Cross-examination continued. I have made no application to the prisoner to make some settlement on my sister since his second marriage; some other members of the family may have done so; I did not instruct the attorney who appears in these proceedings; I did not employ him, but some of the rest of the family did; this prosecution would not have been instituted had he made a settlement on my sister, it being instituted in order to get a provision for his wife.

John Harper re-examined - I am parish clerk of Great Torrington and was present at the marriage of the prisoner with Eliza Stone; the ceremony took place on the 21st of March 1839; I produce a copy of the registry. (The copy was here, put in and read.)

Cross-examined - I have known the prisoner and Eliza Stone for many years; she has been living with her father near Hartland.

Robert Bailey examined - I am a carpenter, living at Hartland. In the year 1832, I went out in the same vessel with Mary Prust to America; we sailed from Devonport on the 28th of March; on the 10th of May following, we landed at Quebec; afterwards saw Mary Prust at Port Hope; she told me she was living with her brother; I remained in Canada 18 months, and then returned to this country; I went home to Hartland, and saw Mary Prust's family; they were living at the West Country Inn; it was two or three years after my return before I had any conversation with Prust; while taking a pint of beer with him, at the King's Arms, I had some conversation with Mr Prust about his wife; I told him I had seen her at Port Hope; Mr Prust said he never wished to see her more; this conversation took place about four years ago; I cannot be precise to the time, but that is about it. I gave him to understand that I had seen her about six weeks before I left America.
Cross-examined by Mr Cockburn - I went to Canada as an emigrant; I am not related to the family of the Prust's but am acquainted with them; do not know where the prisoner was living when I returned.
Did you not meet him at the King's Arms before you had the conversation with him you spoke of? I may have done so several times.
But never spoke to him before about his wife? Never.
I think it singular that since you had seen his wife in Canada, you had not spoken to him about her. I wondered why he did not ask me about her.

Well, and how did this conversation commence - did you begin it, or did he? Prust asked me whether I thought there had been any harm between Capt. Harper and his wife.

That was the captain of the emigrant vessel, I believe, and what was your answer? I said I thought there had not.

Did you not tell him that she was admitted into Captain Harper's cabin? I did.

Admitted when no one was present except themselves. Yes.

And you thought there was no harm in that? I thought it was very strange and wondered at it at the time.

And pray at what time did you cease to wonder at it? She told me afterwards in Canada that she was admitted into the captain's cabin by the direction of the owners of the vessel because she had no friend on board. And that satisfied you? It did.

Then I can only tell you that you are a happy man and very easily satisfied - (laughter). But pray, was this favour conceded to any besides Mrs Prust? It was not.

Then there was no other female without a friend in the vessel besides Mrs Prust? Oh! Yes, there was - there was another young woman from the same parts who was admitted into the captain's cabin - (laughter).

And pray, what might her name be? Margaret Trick (laughter).

So, then Miss Trick had no other friend on the ship except the captain? I believe she had not.

She occasionally shared the honour with Mrs Prust of a private audience with the captain in his own cabin. She did.

Benjamin Yeo, examined - I reside at Hartland, and at one time lived on the estate of the prisoner; I left about twelve months back; I knew the prisoner's wife quite well; about nine months after she left him, I had a conversation with Prust respecting his wife; I told him that a letter had been received from her; and he replied that he knew it; I said there is no telling, but perhaps some- day or other you may come together again; ***"he said, I hope not, I hope never to see her again, so help me God."***

This was the Case for the Prosecution.

Mr Cockburn then proceeded to address the jury on behalf of the prisoner. He commenced by remarking that although the statute, in general, made it illegal for a man to marry again whilst his first wife was living, yet there was one exception to this rule - for the statute declared that it was not criminal for a man to contract a second marriage, if the wife had been absent from her husband for seven years, without his having knowledge of her being alive. There was one general rule in cases of this description, to which the present proceeding formed a most remarkable exception. The rule was that the prosecution was instituted by the friends of the second wife. But here, the second wife, a very respectable young woman, did not come forward to call down the vengeance of the law upon the accused; she had no resentment; she did not feel that the prisoner had done her any wrong. But who was it that had come forward to prosecute? Why it was the friends of the first wife - of that wife to whom he had no wrong - but who had embittered his life, whom even her own friends would not keep at home, but who had been sent out by them in the mixed company of an emigrant ship, unprotected - no, not unprotected, but consigned to the friendship of a man who, it appeared, was at once the captain of the ship and the ship's husband - (loud laughter). After what they had heard of her conduct during that voyage, could they not readily imagine what a **Turk and Tartar of a wife she must have been** - sure he was that in whatever position their verdict might place him, she had absconded from her husband's roof and fled her acquaintance (they had heard how she had beguiled the tedium of a sea voyage), and she had suffered, without one sigh or longing lingering look for a home, she had suffered for seven long years the broad waters of the Atlantic to roll between her and her husband, when he, bold man, on one bright morning, oblivious of all the miseries he had endured from womankind, with chivalrous adventure dared once more to link his fortunes with a female. Scorching, nay downright burning, will not teach some people to keep their fingers out of the fire - some men could not be taught by any lessons, by any experience, however bitter. Now he is married, we've got him, says this woman's friends; the news flies to America, and the woman hastens back, her breast beating high with the hope that if she could not torment at a distance, she might torment him at home. **But she came not to seek the restitution of conjugal rights - oh no! She came after money,** she sought not his love, but she loved his hard cash, and she sought as the fair, just, and legitimate return of all the misery she had accumulated upon him, that he should do what? Why!

Make a handsome settlement upon her for life. That extortion the prisoner very properly resisted, and hence the present proceeding.

The Chairman said he had stopped the evidence, which was intended to show cruelty on the part of the husband as a justification for the wife's leaving her home, and he should now tell them to take no notice whatever of the observations which had just been addressed to them by the learned Counsel as to her conduct either before or after she left her home, the question being narrowed into a very small circle, did he or did he not know that she was alive at any time within seven years before his last marriage, if he did not his conduct came within the exception of the statute, if he did, then he had been guilty of the charge laid against him.
The Jury, after remaining in deliberation for ten minutes, returned a verdict of:

Not Guilty

Thomas Prust and his wife, Eliza Stone, had eleven children, who in turn went on to produce more children.

l) The twelfth child of Thomas Prust and Sarah Ching, his wife was **Edward Prust**, also brother to the above Thomas Prust. He was baptised at Hartland on 23 February **1810** and buried on 28 October **1826,** aged 16 years.

** **Daniel Prust,** the eighth son of Thomas Prust and Sarah Ching (re: J on page 77), was baptised at Hartland on the 20 March **1808**. He

married **Grace Foot Rowe** on 22 May **1830**.

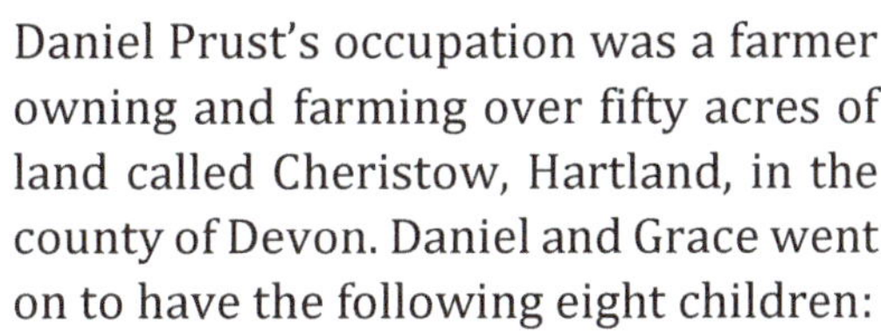
Daniel Prust's occupation was a farmer owning and farming over fifty acres of land called Cheristow, Hartland, in the county of Devon. Daniel and Grace went on to have the following eight children:

1) **Daniel Prust,** born **1827-1905**

2) **Nora Foot Prust,** born **1832-1922**

3) **William Edward Prust**, born in **1835** at Hartland and died in **1871** at the London Hospital, Whitechapel, London, aged 36 years old.

4) **Charles Henry Prust**, born **1837-1917**

5) **Emma Prust,** born in **1839,** she married **Nathaniel Jenkins**. She died in **1913**

6) **George Henry Prust**. Born **1840-1922**, married **Mary Ann Turner,** and they had six children.

7) **Edwin Prust.** Born **1844-1860,** and lastly,

8) **Sarah Ann Prust,** Born in **1847,** she married **John Riley** and had three children and then married Thomas Howarth. Sarah Ann died in **1907**.

Daniel Prust and his wife, Grace Foot Rowe, are buried in the graveyard of their parish church of Saint Nectan in Hartland, Devon. Upon his death, his son George Henry Prust inherited the farm according to Kelly's Directories of Devon, George H Prust was residing as a farmer at Cheristow, Hartland, near Bideford, in Devon.

Back to the children of Daniel Prust and his wife, Grace Foot Rowe.

Their eldest son of Daniel and Grace Foot Rowe was also called Daniel, and he was born in the year **1827** and died in **1906.** This is what is known of Daniel Prust from records and some information from his family in America.

Daniel Prust * 1827-1905

Daniel, according to the census records, was an apprentice and the only employee working for Mr. William Ashton in Hartland, Devon, as a shoe and harness maker for horses. It is known that he had a falling out with his father and decided to emigrate. Daniel later left England in 1860, embarking from Plymouth for Quebec and arriving in Detroit in the United States of America in March of **1860** to start a new life. He later settled in Indiana. Daniel went back to the trade he knew when he was in England, which was as a shoe and harness maker. Although disliking this trade, he worked hard and managed to save enough money to buy an 80-acre farm near Walnut Prairie in York Township. He married **Lydia Balthis** of Corydon, Indiana, in 1860. Daniel Prust became a nationalized citizen in October 1865. They went on to have eight children. Three sons and five daughters. The children were Elizabeth Prust Baker, William, Daniel, Emma Prust Manhart, Nora Prust Edwards, Harry, and Ola Prust Manhart, they lost an infant daughter called Grace, who is buried in Rockville, Indiana. Daniel built his house and barn in 1865. He later acquired several hundred acres of land and divided it amongst his children.

A 1902 photograph shows the Daniel Prust family at the Prust homestead. (Submitted by Jewell Manhart Kile)

Daniel Prust died in Clark County, Illinois, in **1905,** aged 78 years. His wife died when she was 89 years old, and they are both buried in Walnut Prairie Cemetery, Indiana. U.S.A.

3) **John Prust,** third son of Joseph and Grace Galsworthy baptised at Hartland on 26 July **1696**. He was the executor of his father's will and had residue of his estate.

4) **Thomas Prust,** the fourth son of Joseph and his wife, Grace Galsworthy. He was known as '**Thomas Prust of Milford,'** He was baptised at Hartland on the 4 March **1690**. He was of Milford in Hartland and was named in his father's will.

Thomas Prust married at Hartland on the 6th of May **1733** to **Elizabeth Harris.** Thomas Prust died in his 88th year, and he was buried at Hartland on 13 January **1778.** The following is an abstract from his will dated 26 July 1771.

<u>This is the Will of Thomas Prust 1690-1778</u>

He gives his daughter Grace Prust £10 twelve months after his decease.
Gives each of his other daughters (no names) 1/- each.
Gives to his son Thomas Prust 1/- (One Shilling).

Gives to each of his grandchildren 1/-. Gives to his daughter Mary Fish (over and above the 1/-) £3.3.0 one year after his decease.
Residue to his wife Elizabeth Prust as long as she continues a widow and makes her executrix for the same period.
The will was proved at Barnstable by Elizabeth Prust the widow on the 3rd of Feb. 1778.

Note his eldest son Thomas only received one shilling in his will, but when his widow Elizabeth Prust died three years later in **1781,** her will (which was proved on the 3rd of May 1781) was more generous than her husband's. The following is an abstract from her will. Dated 7 January **1780.**

<u>This is the Will of Elizabeth Prust (nee Harris), Wife of Thomas Prust</u>

Elizabeth Prust of the parish of Hartland, Devon, and widow. Dated 7 January 1780 *"Gives daughter in law Ann Prust 40/- Gives to grandchildren John, William, Thomas & Ann Prust 20/- each. Gives to daughter Elizabeth Bowman 40/-Gives to daughter Grace King 20/- and gives to son-in-law Thomas King 20/- in trust for his daughter Ursula. Gives to grandchildren Margaret, Elizabeth & William Fish 20/- each, and gives to friend Mr. Thomas Galsworthy the younger, of Moor, £3 in trust for granddaughter Ann Hamblyn, so that the same or any part of thereof might not be in the hands of her mother or present husband. Gives residue of her estate to daughter Mary Cloutman and makes her executrix. Before executing will she gives her grandson William Hamblyn 20/- to be paid to his grandmother Mrs. Hamblyn of Stoke."*

Witness, Thomas Velly.

The seal of her will has a crest of a unicorn's head.

5) **Mary Prust,** daughter of Joseph Prust and Grace Galsworthy, baptised, at Hartland on 6 September **1677**. She is named in the will of her grandfather Mr. Joseph Prust. She married there on the 1 June 1710 to **Robert Mugford** Esq.

6) **Grace Prust**, daughter of Joseph Prust and Grace Galsworthy, she was baptised at Hartland on 9 February **1687** and named in her father's will, giving her a sum of £20 two years after her 21st birthday. Grace married **John Beer** in 1716.

A Change of Name to Prust

Joseph Prust Hamlyn, who was born in the year **1758** and died as **Joseph Prust Prust** in the year **1807,** Joseph Prust Hamlyn was the son of the Reverend Robert Hamlyn and his wife **Judith Prust**; she was the daughter of William and Elizabeth Prust of Bideford in Devon.

Joseph was sent to further his education at Exeter College in Devon and matriculated in **1775** but remained in the college as a commoner (not on a scholarship) until he was 21 in **1779**. This was the year that he decided to change his surname from Hamlyn to Prust, and it was also the year that his mother Judith died, and his father remarried a young girl called Francis Collins, which must have caused much distress to Joseph and the Prust family. Judith and Robert Hamlyn had three sons, Joseph, Robert, and William Hamlyn, but Joseph's other brothers retained their original surname of Hamlyn. I can speculate that there is some more evidence that there was a family rift between the Hamlyn and the Prust families, as there is a will by Elizabeth Prust dated **1780** that she bequeaths a small sum of money in trust for her young granddaughter Ann Hamlyn to be held in trust by Thomas Galsworthy with the proviso ***" that same or any part thereof might not be in the hands of her mother or present husband"*** there was another bequest by Elizabeth which she gives to her grandson William Hamlyn the sum of twenty shillings ***"to be paid to his grandmother Mrs. Hamlyn of Stoke"*** (see page 86), So we know that in 1779 the year of his mother Judith's death, his father's remarriage and the year that he left Exeter College.

When Joseph changed his name from Hamlyn to **PRUST,** he was known thereafter as Joseph Prust Prust; he later became The **Reverend Joseph Prust Prust.** Above is a plaque in memory and honour of the Rev. Joseph Prust Prust, this includes members of his family, sons, and daughters. This plaque is on the wall of St. Hallows church of Woolfardisworthy (also called Woolsey) in the county of Devon, and information is included in the Woolsery history and guide booklet. This church was originally a chapelry dependent on the parish church of Hartland and became separated during the Reformation. The porch and font are Norman, and the tower is the only example from as early as the 13th century in north Devon.

In **1780** Joseph married a lady called **Susanna Silke** of Bideford in Devon.

Joseph and Susanna went on to have eleven children. Their eldest child was also called Joseph Prust Prust, born one year later in **1781-1839,** and he also entered the clergy. Their other children were Elizabeth, Susanna, Robert, Judith, John, Sarah Waxman, Mary, Jane Silke, Bartholomew, and Thomas.

Bartholomew Prust and the Ship Hms Bellophon

The third son of Joseph Prust Prust and his wife Susanna was **Bartholomew Prust,** who was born in **1796**. Bartholomew entered The Royal Navy; he held the title of a Lieutenant on the ship the 'HMS Bellerophon' dated 1805. Picture shown below.

This picture is inscribed with the words:

'Situation of the Bellerophon at the moment of the death of her gallant commander Capt. Cooke October 21st, 1805'

Bartholomew Prust joined the Royal Navy and went to sea in 1810 when he was only 14 years old. He was a midshipman and later was made a Commissioned Officer on the 25th of May **1822** when he was 26 years old. He served on the 'HMS Bellerophon,' which was a third-rate ship of the line of the Royal Navy. The Bellerophon was launched in 1786 and served during the French Revolutionary and The Napoleonic Wars.

'HMS Bellerophon' was also known to sailors as the "Billy Ruffian" she fought in three fleet actions, the Glorious First of June, the Battle of the Nile, and was also the ship Napoleon finally surrendered aboard, ending nearly 22 years of war with France. She was detached to reinforce Rear-Admiral Horatio Nelson's fleet in 1798 and took part in the decisive defeat of a French fleet at the Battle of the Nile.

'Bellerophon' returned to European waters with the resumption of the wars with France.

The reinforced fleet, then commanded by **Horatio Nelson 1758-1805**, engaged the combined Franco-Spanish fleet when it emerged from the port.

At the historic 'Battle of Trafalgar' on the day of the 21st of October 1805, 'Bellerophon' fought a bitter engagement against Spanish and French ships, sustaining heavy casualties and losing to death their Captain Cook. In 1815 she was assigned to blockade the French Atlantic port of Rochefort, and in July 1815, Napoleon was defeated at Waterloo, and finding escape to America was barred by the blockading Bellerophon and other ships. Napoleon came aboard "the ship that had dogged his steps for twenty years" to finally surrender to the British. It was Bellerophon's last seagoing service as she was paid off and converted to a prison ship in **1815** and was renamed 'Captivity' in 1824. Bellerophon's long and distinguished career has been recorded in literature and folk songs, commemorating the achievements of the "Billy Ruffian". On retiring from the navy, Bartholomew went on to become a Magistrate for the County of Devon.

Bartholomew later married Miss **Elizabeth Susanna Burgh** in 1827 in Westminster, London. They had no issues.
Below is a memorial plaque that is in All Hallows church at Woolfardisworthy in the county of Devon. Bartholomew died in 1862, and his wife Elizabeth died twenty years later in 1882 and left over four thousand pounds to her solicitor Mr. T. J. P. Tucker

Thomas Prust (Re: page 85) 1690-1778 and **Elizabeth Harris,** his wife, had the following four children:

a) **Thomas Prust 1738-1780** He was also known as '**Thomas Prust of Mugford'.** By the smallest of Legacy he received under his father's will, namely 1/- (one shilling), father and son had not agreed. Thomas Prust was baptised at Hartland on 16 April **1738.** He married a Miss **Anne Ashton**, and she is mentioned in the will of her mother-in-law Elizabeth Prust as the widow of her son Thomas. (refer to page 87).

Though the following record from 'The National Archives ref: QS/1/3/429'' it was found that Thomas Prust was also the Master of a sloop called '***The John of Bristol.'*** (A sloop is a sailboat with a single mast, typically having only one headsail in front of the mast and one mainsail aft of (behind) the mast. Such an arrangement was called a fore-and-aft rig).

The following is from a newspaper article of the time:

Thomas Prust, master, and Richard White, mariner, both of the sloop John of Bristol, testified that they shipped, at Bristol in December 1771, 480 bushels of white salt, duty paid, to be carried to Falmouth and Truro for Philip Westcott, Thomas Barker and William Dyer of Falmouth, and Joseph Ferris, Richard Jewell, and William Harpur of Truro. The sloop was driven into Carmarthen Bay, South Wales, on 15 January, in a violent storm, and sank with the loss of the entire cargo. But his crew were reported to be rescued from this storm.

Thomas Prust died and was buried at Hartland there on 11 August. 1780. Anne Prust, his wife, died just two months later and was buried at Hartland on the 6 October. 1780.
The four children of Thomas Prust and Ann Ashton, his wife, were:
A) **William Prust,** baptised at Hartland on 1 November **1767** and was named in the wills of his grandfather and his grandmother.
B) **Anne Prust,** baptised in **1769,** place unknown she was named in the wills of her grandparents Thomas Prust and his wife, Elizabeth Harris. Ann Prust married a **Mr. Hamblyn** Esquire.

C) **John Prust** was born in about **1770**. Neither he nor his brother Thomas or his sister Anne were baptised at Hartland but elsewhere. John is named in the wills of his grandfather and Grandmother, Thomas & Elizabeth Prust. Mr. John Prust married at Hartland on the 30 December **1785** to Miss **Elizabeth Score**, by whom he had four children, three daughters and a son as follows: -

William Prust, baptised at Hartland on 11 January **1789****
Sarah Prust, baptised at Hartland on 15 October **1786.**
Elizabeth Prust, baptised at Harland on 6 January **1788.**
Grace Prust, baptised at Hartland on 7 February **1795.**

D) **Thomas Prust**, son of Thomas & Anne, was born about 1772 and named in the Wills of his Grandparents. He married first on the 29 August **1794** to Miss **Joanna Cruse** and secondly at Clovelly on the 13 September **1804** to Miss **Mary Medland** of Clovelly. Mr. Thomas Prust resided at Welcome. By his second wife Mary (nee Medland), there was a former connection between the Prust's and Medland's for Mr. Thomas Prust, the kinsman of Mr. John Prust, by his will, proved 2 Aug. **1711**, gives to his wife her heirs and assigns forever, all messuages, etc., in Great Torrington, Devon, then in possession of John Medland

The second child of Thomas Prust and his wife Elizabeth Harris was:

b) **Mary Prust,** baptised at Hartland on 16 April **1734** and married there on 17 May **1752** to Mr. **William Fish** and had three children Margaret, Elizabeth, and William Fish. Mary is named in her grandfather's will, and her children in that of her mother's will. She married secondly to Mr. **Thomas Cloutman in 1774,** whereupon she received the residue of her mother Elizabeth Prust's estate (page 87) and went on to have a further two children, Robert Cloutman and Thomas Cloutman.

The third child of Thomas Prust and his wife Elizabeth Harris was:

c) **Grace Prust**, baptised at Hartland on 21 May **1736**, was named in her father's will and with her husband in her mother's will. She married at Hartland on 13 April 1778 to Mr. **Thomas King,** by whom she had a daughter Ursula King who was named in her fathers will.

The fourth child of Thomas Prust and his wife, Elizabeth, was a daughter also named after her mother.

d) **Elizabeth Prust,** baptised at Hartland in September of **1742** and named in her mother's will, married **Mr. Bowman.**

** Following on from the son of John Prust and Elizabeth Score (3), his wife (see page 93) **William Prust** (Draper), who was born in **1789** in Hartland. He married **Sarah Burnard**. William had the occupation of a Carpenter and Draper in 1841. The family lived in Harton Village in Hartland, Devon. He later became a Draper and Grocer. (To differentiate between people of the same name, I have added the suffix of their occupation) therefore, I will call him William Prust (Draper). Note that his son William (1819) refers to him also as a Draper; see image on the following page. The family business was profitable, so they were comfortable off and employed a few servants. William and Sarah had the following six children.

1) **William Prust 1819-1874**. (Vitualler) William went to London and became a Licensed Vitualler. He married **Miss Alice Brown**, and

together, they ran a public house in Poplar, East London, called 'The Woolsack.' When William Prust died in 1879, his wife Alice continued to run the pub until she died three years later in 1877. They had no children.

The document below is a certificate of 'Freedom of the City' dated 14th October **1859** referring to William Prust Vitualler at the Ball & Bush PH.

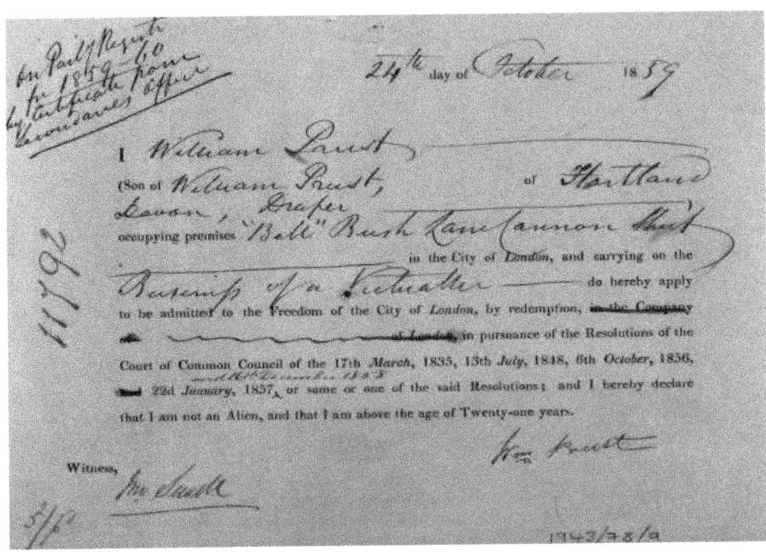

24th day of October 1859

I William Prust

(Son of William Prust, of Hartland Devon, Draper)

occupying premises "Ball" Bush Lane Cannon Street in the City of London, and carrying on the Business of a Victualler do hereby apply to be admitted to the Freedom of the City of London, by redemption, ~~in the Company of London,~~ in pursuance of the Resolutions of the Court of Common Council of the 17th *March*, 1835, 13th *July*, 1848, 6th *October*, 1856, ~~and~~ 22d *January*, 1857, or some or one of the said Resolutions; and I hereby declare that I am not an Alien, and that I am above the age of Twenty-one years.

Wm Prust

Witness,

11792

5/6

1943/78/a

1) **Elizabeth Prust 1820-1874.** Elizabeth never married and termed herself as a Draper, working in the family business.

2) **Richard Burnard Prust, 1829-1896,** was the second son of William Prust (Draper) and his wife, Sarah Burnard. Richard married **Margaret Elizabeth Way.** Richard and Margaret lived in the Manor House at Hartland and went on to have nine children. Pictured on the left is Richard Prust, taken from a local book on Hartland, Devon. The text from this book quotes the following:

"Richard Prust as well as farming owned Docton Mill, Gorrans Down, Elmtree, Coopers Court Cottage and in Fore Street Nos. 13,14,25,27,29,40, and 43. The wooden perambulator was built by a local craftsman for

Richard and Margaret Prust of The Manor House for their nine children. It was last used in 1875 for Michael Ernest Prust whose son Horace is the last male descendant of the Prust line. A family indigenous to Hartland for 700 years. It is believed that these three wheeled prams were the first to be used in the parish."

3) **Mary Jane Prust 1830-1917** Mary Jane also never married and referred to herself as a Draper working in the family business and later a retired Draper with a live-in servant until she died aged 87 years old. In her will, Mary Jane left just under seven thousand pounds to be shared between her Niece, Henrietta S. A. Burrow, and her Nephew, John William Prust Burrow.

4) **Fanny Prust 1832-1911.** Fanny married **William Burrows,** a farmer in Hartland, and had two children: Henrietta Sarah Ann Burrow and John William Prust Burrow. The family later moved to Cornwall.

5) **Sarah Prust 1837-1883.** Sarah Ann married William T **Ellacott,** a Stockbroker who came from Cornwall. The family later moved to Surrey (also known as 'the stockbroker's belt'), whereupon they had one son called William Prust Ellacott. His occupation was of a 'Gentleman' according to his marriage certificate. William married twice and eventually settled in Torridge near Hartland in Devon.

Prust's who attended Oxford University

There was a 'Thomas le Prust' in 1273. Abraham Prust, son of Hugh of Monkleigh, Devon (gent.) Exeter College, matric. 1638-9 age 16 years. Hugh Prust, son of Thomas of Halton, Devon (gent.) Wadham College, matric 1669-70, age 17; buried in the college chapel 1671. John Prust B.A. 1531. Joseph Prust, son of Joseph of Monkleigh, Devon (gent.) Balliol College, matric 1677 age 18. Joseph Prust, son of Thomas of Woolfardisworthy, Devon (gent.). St. Mary Hall, matric 1679-80. B.A. age 17, B.A.

Hartland: Prust's Plot at High Farford

Farford farm as it is today.

There was a piece of land in High Farford in Hartland called 'Prust Plot.' The history of High Farford is that in the year **1702,** Henry Bagelhole granted the lease on a Platt (as it was known then) at the bottom of Gleanings Parke to **Edmund Prust** to be held during the lives of Edmund and Ulalia Prust and together with Alice Prust, their daughter. On this land, Edmund Prust built a cottage, and the plot which formed his garden is still known as Prust's Plot. The field on the opposite side of the road is known as Alice's meadow. The banks in that area are a mass of primroses and bluebells in the spring as if someone has made a significant effort to make it prettier than elsewhere. Edmund and Ulalia were also the great-grandparents of Stephen Prust of Bristol, Ship owner, merchant, and philanthropist.

Stephen Prust of Bristol 1771-1850

Included here is a Clipper sailing ship and the halfpenny coin of 1795 to represent the life of Stephen Prust when he was a young man of 24 years old. The coin because he was fond of it, being a businessman and merchant, and the ship because he was a sea captain and, as such, had a close affinity with the sea together with his business of sailing ships of the time.

This advertisement which was in the local Bristol paper was offering freight or passage for his ship 'The Europa.'

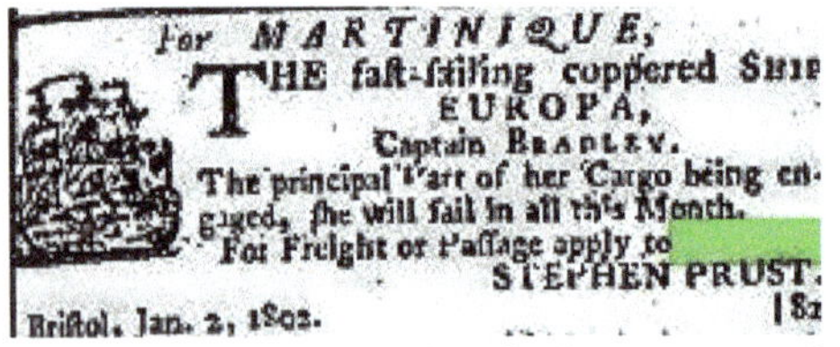

For MARTINIQUE,

THE faſt-ſailing coppered Ship
EUROPA,
Captain BRADLEY.

The principal Part of her Cargo being engaged, ſhe will ſail in all this Month.

For Freight or Paſſage apply to
STEPHEN PRUST.

Briſtol, Jan. 2, 1802.

Stephen Prust was born in Bristol in **1771**, and he was one of nine or ten children and the son of Captain Edmund Prust 1742-1789 and his wife, Elizabeth Jose, both of whom were from Cornwall.

His father was Captain Edmund Prust, and his uncle was Thomas Prust, both born about 1745, and both Mariners**.** Thomas Prust was the captain of a boat called 'The John of Bristol,' and he married twice. His first wife was Sarah Wood in 1772, and secondly, he married Elizabeth Thomas on Christmas Day in 1775. Stephen's cousin was William Prust of Bristol, the customs house officer.

Stephen was the only surviving male child to make it to adulthood. Although he had six sisters, five also survived to adulthood, and all married well, especially his favourite closest sister, Sophia: This is some of what is known and recorded of his sister **Sophia Prust.** She was born in Bristol in **1774,** and she was mentioned in her brother Stephen's will. She married **Captain Matthew Stewart** in Bristol in 1806. He was born in 1770 and was the son of the Reverend Charles Stewart of Kintyre, Argyllshire, Scotland. The couple emigrated to Quebec in Canada.

They settled in Nouvelle, Quebec, and then went on to St. John's Island (later, it was renamed **Prince Edwards Island**) in 1792.

In 1813 Captain Matthew was the master of a ship called 'Mary' (maybe after 'Mary, Queen of Scots, who married Lord Darnley). This ship was built at Darnley, Glasgow, in Scotland, and later was reported to be raided and captured by American privateers. Matthew and Sophia Stewart owned many thousands of acres of land, and Matthew, who was described as a 'Merchant' of Saint-Omer, purchased the land from 'The Shoolbred Seigniory' in **1809**.

Information regarding 'The Shoolbred Seigniory'

After the English victory (The battle of Quebec) against the French, British soldiers seized the colony. In those days, loyal service to the King was repaid with grants of land and seigniories. It was probably for services rendered that an English merchant by the name of John Shoolbred was offered, in 1788, land in the Gaspé Peninsula that eventually carried the name of the Seigniory of Shoolbred. A seignior owned the lands, and even if he did not reside in the area, he received an annual rent from the citizens who did. Back to Stephen Prust of Bristol, who had many business interests: He was chair of the Temperance committee and wrote many letters to the editor of the Bristol newspapers regarding the famine in Ireland and made donations to the Methodist missions. Stephen was also an enthusiastic non-conformist and was also a member of the Bristol Missionary Society. He was known to do good work and be involved in many worthy causes, but I have recently found that Stephen was also involved in the **slave trade;** this fact was not mentioned in his obituary. Stephen was also on the list of members of the board of the famous Bristol Tobacconists W. D & H. O Wills, who were his good friends and non-Conformists. W.D. was short for William Day, and H. O. short for Henry Overton.

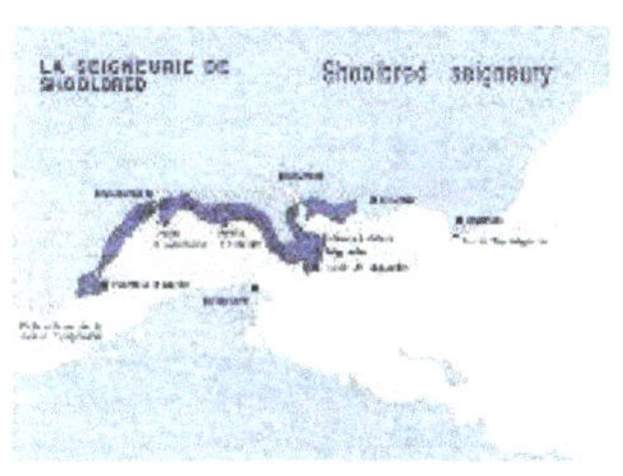

Henry Overton Wills named his son after his best friend, so naming him 'Stephen Prust Wills.' Through further research, it has been found that Stephen Prust, 'Merchant', had an interest in the ships called *'Allison,' 'Bacchus'* & *'Robust.'* It is recorded that these ships were used for importing various goods but were also used in the slave trade! As in **1799,** Stephen owned a boat called 'Allison'. There is evidence that this vessel stopped off in Angola to pick up slaves and arrived in Martinique with 375 slaves on board; from there, 289 slaves were taken to Jamaica to work in British-owned plantations.

Stephen was also known to own a ship called 'Bacchus' that ship went to Barbados and Jamaica. *(Sources: Bristol Presentments 1802, 1806, African accounts No.4; 1800 & Bristol Presentments 1806).* On the journey back, he took on Tobacco for his good friends W.D & H O Wills, the owners of the famous Bristol Tobacco company in England, who were also involved in the slave trade, as were many other prominent merchants in Bristol at that time.

Stephen Prust married Miss Sarah Summers; in **1804,** she was the daughter of William Summers, a Gentleman of Westminster, London. Stephen was 33 years old, and Sarah was just 20 years old. William Summers gave his lawful consent as the natural father of Sarah Summers, who was a minor at the time, being under twenty-one. In **1812** Stephen's wife Sarah died of consumption. Stephen and Sarah had three children. **Stephen Summer Prust** was born in **1805.** He attended Oxford University to study law, whereupon he sadly passed away in his 17th year at 'Thatcher's' Oxford University in Berkshire in **1821**. Stephen had much personal heartbreak in his life as not only did he lose his wife but his son and only daughter Emily Prust died before him.

Edmund Thornton Prust, pictured here, was born in the year **1808,** a handsome young man; he was the second son of Stephen Prust. He also went to university and then became a Methodist minister of a church in Northamptonshire; he was also on a list of ministers and clergy in 1841. Edmund married **Mary Ann Randel,** and they had two sons who sadly both died in infancy. The painting of Edmund Prust is in a private collection today in Australia, and his family has given their kind permission for it to be reproduced for this book. Edmund wrote this book of *sermons* printed in 1879 which is still available today.

(Source census 1841, data supplied by Alan Clark).

Emily Elizabeth Prust was born in **1810-1838**. She was the only daughter of Stephen and Sarah. Emily married her cousin on her grandmother's side Mr **Thomas Porter Jose.** He was a rich industrialist also residing in Bristol and head of the firm T.P. Jose & sons, tobacco merchants of Queen's Square, Bristol.

Thomas Jose later became mayor of Bristol in 1863 and was in the tobacco trade. The picture of 'Thomas Porter Jose' is shown here. Emily and Thomas had four children: Stephen Prust Jose, who became The Rev. **Stephen Prust Jose**, M.A. of Pembroke College, in Oxford. He became the vicar of 'Churchill' in Somerset. William Wilberforce Jose, Emily Mary Jose, and Edmund Jose were the other children. Sadly, Emily died in childbirth together with her baby son Edmund in **1838.** His son-in-law Thomas Jose remarried in 1841 to Isabella Cook and went on to have another family. When Thomas Jose died in 1875, he left twenty-five thousand pounds to his second wife Isabella (which, in today's money this amount is worth over **twenty million pounds),** their children, and his sons Stephen Prust Jose and William Wilberforce Jose were the executors of his will.

Stephen Prust of Bristol had a long life and died in the year **1850,** aged 79 years, and was buried in the family vault of St. James in Bristol. 'Deeply lamented by his family and friends,' so his obituary states.
This is a small excerpt of the will of Stephen Prust of Bristol: In his will, he gave: *freehold farmland and hereditaments of Chapel Allerton and Stone Allerton in Somersetshire to his dear friends William Day Wills and Henry Overton Wills of Bristol Tobacconists. I give to the said William Day Wills and Henry Overton Wills, and my son Edmund Thornton Prust the sum of £6000 upon trust to pay an annual income there from of the securities where in the fund may be invested and waived to my said son Edmund Thornton Prust during his life, etc. Also, I have stock of six percent of the Midland Railway Company I intend purchase more of that stock which I give to the said William Day Wills, Henry Overton Wills and Edmund Thornton Prust six per cent consolidated Bristol & Birmingham etc. I also leave trust funds for my grandchildren Stephen Prust Jose, William Wilberforce Jose, and Mary Emily Jose. (A codicil was added as to his granddaughter, that the trust was to be used for her lifetime and independent of any husband and the same may not be subject to his control, debts, or engagements). I give to my sister Sophia of British Columbia, (Canada) one thousand pounds as a token of my fraternal regard. I give to my sister Patty the wife of the reverend William Thorn of Wincanton one thousand pounds; I give to my sister Betsey Jose Prust one thousand pounds. Which three legacies to be paid to my three sisters respectively, free from the control debts or engagements of any husband. In the case of the decease of my sister Sophia in my lifetime I give the sum of one thousand pounds to each of her seven children or such as shall be living at my decease. I give to my cousin Mary Ball of Bristol one hundred pounds and to her sister Lydia Prust Waite, spinster, one hundred pounds. I give to the said William Day Wills and Henry Overton Wills one hundred pounds and to their brother Frederick Wills fifty pounds.*

It is interesting that he states in his will that his three sisters were given money from the will, free from the control of any husbands, as at that time, women's finances were under the control of their respective husbands. Before 1870 when the women's property act came into force, any money made by a woman either through a wage, from investment, by gift, or through inheritance automatically became the property of her husband once she was married, with the exception of the Dowry.

(Note: £1,000 in 1850 is worth today's value as approximately £60,000).

The Slave Trade and 18th-19th Century Bristol

The above picture shows several indoor slaves on a plantation with their three mistresses in the front.

Bristol was a large trading port overtaking London and Liverpool, trading goods, including slaves, which was a lucrative commodity at that time.

The anti-slavery movement scored its first major victory during the Napoleonic Wars of **1799-1815**, when the British government outlawed the transport of **slaves in ships**, but not the complete abolishment. Under increasing pressure from the British abolitionist movement, the British government enacted the Slave Trade Act in 1807, which abolished the slave trade in the empire. In 1808, Sierra Leone was designated an official British colony for freed slaves. The eminent **William Wilberforce MP** was a prominent leader against the slavery movement at the time to abolish this slave trade.

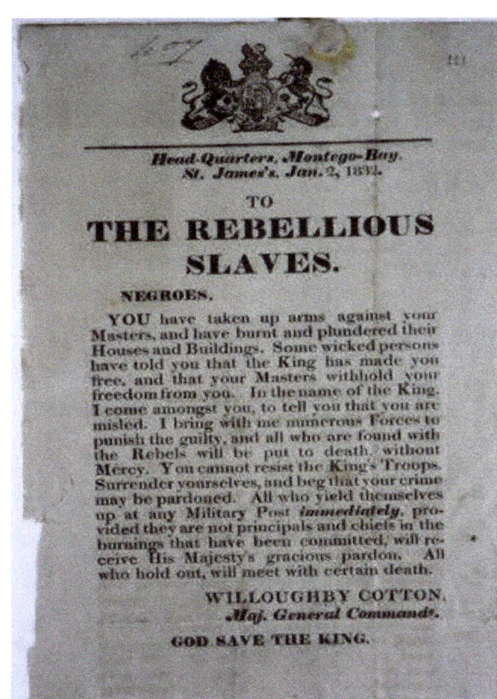

Head-Quarters, Montego-Bay.
St. James's, Jan. 2, 1832.

TO

THE REBELLIOUS SLAVES.

NEGROES,

YOU have taken up arms against your Masters, and have burnt and plundered their Houses and Buildings. Some wicked persons have told you that the King has made you free, and that your Masters withhold your freedom from you. In the name of the King, I come amongst you, to tell you that you are misled. I bring with me numerous Forces to punish the guilty, and all who are found with the Rebels will be put to death, without Mercy. You cannot resist the King's Troops. Surrender yourselves, and beg that your crime may be pardoned. All who yield themselves up at any Military Post *immediately*, provided they are not principals and chiefs in the burnings that have been committed, will receive His Majesty's gracious pardon. All who hold out, will meet with certain death.

WILLOUGHBY COTTON,
Maj. General Command^{g}.

GOD SAVE THE KING.

This poster, dated 1832, is from Jamaica warning slaves who took up arms against their masters who thought that they were free, stating that the rebels will be put to death.

William Wilberforce, who died in the year 1833, sadly was not able to see the emancipation act passed. Interestingly, the grandson of Stephen Prust of Bristol was named after this eminent Member of Parliament. William Wilberforce Jose was born in 1833. This seems a strange connection as William Wilberforce's politics were well known, so what is the connection to the name? We can only guess. Maybe assuming that this man was greatly admired by both Thomas Jose and his wife, Emily Elizabeth Prust Jose, for the naming of their son after him and for his stance in wiping out this abdominal trade that he was so against or maybe something completely different.

Those against the abolition were the ones that had the most to lose and not just the British slave traders, but the heads of some of the African tribes in Africa that used to sell their own people to these privateers._Most ship owners, including Stephen Prust of Bristol and the tobacco merchants, became extraordinarily rich from this trade until the abolition of the slave trade. The bill was finally passed ('the Emancipation Act' of 1834). And to stop the furor of Bristol merchants and plantation owners, who invested in this trade, a compensation scheme was set up for the loss of their enslaved property, giving out the equivalent of billions in reparations in today's money in **1834**.
A debt to generations of British taxpayers finally paid off in 2015.

Another recorded member of the Prust family was **John Prust,** Merchant and Slave Trader. **John Prust** was born in about **1735**, he was also the uncle of Stephen Prust of Bristol, and according to records, it is stated that between the years of **1762-1818,** John Prust was a merchant and slave trader. John Prust picked up slaves from Africa and transported them to 'The Americas' in exchange for produce of sugar, rum, rice, ginger and tobacco. He also used them as sailors on board his ships. According to an amazing document of former British Colonial Dependencies of **1812-1834,** there is a list of the owners and their slaves. This shows that John Prust owned eighteen house slaves in Hanover, Jamaica.

The oldest slave was a 60-year-old negro man called **'Foot'** and a 50-year-old black African called **'Lookout'** the other slaves seem to be in families, as we have a **'Rosy'** a 55-year-old Creole woman who had sons, **William, Ben, Philip,** and daughter '**Veney',** and a 6-year-old son or grandson called '**Rodney'**. Another slave was **'Milly,** a 32-year-old African woman who had two sons. 12-year-old '**Neptune'** and 9-year-old **Bob**.
'**Phoebe'** was a 30-year-old Creole woman with her one-year-old son called **Donas** and a ten-year-old daughter called '**Peachy'.** The other slaves were **Joe, Dago, Rosina,** and two-year-old '**Polydone'** son of Grace.

John Prust was given compensation from the government of the time when the slave trade was abolished in **1833** in Britain.

John Prust had four children, John, Abigale, Mary and Sarah, who became very wealthy, inheriting their father's estate. Abigale Prust (spinster) died in **1828** and left large sums of money from her estate in her will to her nieces, Mary and Elizabeth Prust of Bristol and her niece Sarah Woodbine/Woolbine of London, also a legacy to her nephew **William Prust** (gent) son of her late brother John the clear annual sum of one hundred pounds for during the term of his natural life upon the proviso that if he shall not mortgage, sell or otherwise encumber the said annuity of one hundred pounds, whereupon the yearly sum shall cease and no longer be payable to him. You must wonder that Abigale thought her nephew might squander or indeed sell off his inheritance to add that into her will. This William Prust, her nephew, was of White Court Fields in London and died in **1854**. According to his will, he left all his assets to his sister Elizabeth Prust

of Bristol and his sister Sarah Woodbine/Woolbine and her children, John Woodbine and Mary Ann Woodbine. (Records show both spellings of Woolbine and Woodbine)
This concludes the information on The Slaves and the Prust ownership of these people.

Prust Families Of Yorkshire

A NEW HOE AT WORK, GOING BETWEEN THE ROWS OF PLANTS

William Prust, Coachman and Farmer. **1738-1827.**

This is another line of the Prust family that I can trace back to Yorkshire to the 16th century and no further, so it is unsure if this line originated in the parish of Hartland in Devon.

This biography is of some of the earliest Prust families who came from North Yorkshire in the district of Flixton in Yorkshire. There is a small village known as Pickhill-cum-Roxley, which is mainly made up of agricultural farming. The chief crops grown there were Turnips, Wheat, Barley, and Oats.

There is a record that there was a man called 'William Prust' who was born in the area in about 1738 when King George II was on the throne. At the time, there was a chaotic presence within Great Britain due to the last of the Jacobite rebellions being fought around the area. William later travelled south to London, where He eventually obtained the prestigious occupation of being a Coachman for King George II and his entourage. After a few years, he later decided to move back to his roots and journeyed north to Pickhill-cum-Roxley. There he married a woman called **Ann,** and they had a son called **George Prust,** who was born in **1765**. Ann died, and William remarried another woman called **Elizabeth Turner** in **1769** in Pickhill. William and Elizabeth had two sons **Joseph Prust** who, it is known, disappeared to Australia after a family argument and died in Melbourne, leaving considerable wealth.

The second son was called **William Turner Prust,** with the middle name of 'Turner' after his mother.

William Turner Prust 1771-1852

William, born about **1771** who, went on to marry a lady called **Harriet Donkin Walker** in 1802. William's occupation was that of a 'Farmer' this is according to the UK poll book and election register. He was the occupier of land that he rented for upwards of £50 a year, so a fair amount of land.

This William (known as **William Prust senior**) and his wife Harriet had six sons and three daughters. The other known sons were **William, Thomas, Simeon, James, Edward,** and **John Prust.**

According to the 1841 census, William's three sons, Simeon, James, & Edward, were all farming the family farm together with other farm labourers recorded.

The Napoleonic War 1803-1815 Due to the mass conflicts with the French, Britain was at war. William and his sons were working hard to produce more food for the country, and at the same time, The Town Councils around the country were asked to provide an overseer to some of the French soldiers that were captured and had become prisoners of war, putting them to work in the local districts. 33-year-old William was, in fact, drafted in to do this job. A short while later, a posse of French prisoners arrived in the area. Hurriedly, shift accommodation was made to put up to house them around the surrounding farms.

As previously, these prisoners were a massive drain on the British prison system as forced incarceration expanded not only in size but also cost. As a result, the prisoners would be stationed in a small country and market towns from the southern coast all the way up to the Scottish border. Due to the pressures they put on the British economy, the French POWs were forced to do labour, such as digging trenches to aid with drainage. It is recorded that some prisoners had cramped living conditions but with access to good food. There have been letters archived from the French POWs to the British overseers commending them for their treatment towards the POWS when they were released. William put these prisoners to work in Flixton to dig trenches to drain the land. The relationship between our William Prust and the POWs is not known, but it is to be assumed that they were favourable!

William Turner Prust and **Harriet Donkin Walker** had eleven children. Their first son was named:

1) William Prust was born in **1803** and died in **1806** aged three years old

2) William Prust **1806 - 1852**

Their second son was also another 'William' (called William Prust junior). He also married twice, like his father; His first wife was called. After her death in 1846, William junior remarried a lady called Jane Otterbourne, by whom he had four children. William, like his father, according to the UK poll & election register, lived in a freehold house and owned his own land. William and Ann had four children. Elizabeth, Hannah, Edwin, and Eliza Prust.

3) Elizabeth Prust **1809-1819.**

4) Harriet Prust **1810-1864.**

5) John Prust, the fifth child of William Turner Prust and Harriet Donkin Walker, was born about **1814.** Shown below is a photo of him with his second wife, Elizabeth Pinkney. John became a rich cattle

dealer and wealthy Butcher.

It is known that he was corresponding with his uncle in Melbourne, Australia. He married twice; his first wife was Amy Welborne, and in **1827**

and they had a daughter called Amy Prust. With his second wife, Elizabeth Pinkney, they went on to have the following children.

a) Thomas Pinkney Prust 1842-1848,
b) Harriet Prust 1843-1925,
c) Elizabeth Ann Prust 1844-
d) Emma Prust 1847-1849,
e) Emma Prust (2) 1848-1925,

a) Thomas William Prust 1850-1909 is pictured here. He married Sabina Bulmer in 1875. His occupation was a Chemist and Druggist. The family lived in the town of Leeds. After his death, his widow Sabina Prust **emigrated to America** with two of her children, Sabina Daisy Prust 1882-1936 and Minnie Prust 1891-? Her other sons John, Thomas William, and Charles Arthur Prust, had already emigrated previously and were living in **California, U.S.A.**

c) It is known that Charles Arthur Prust fought in World War 1. This sign I came across is from California, so in all probability, this family, after emigrating, opened a bar and grill.

6) The sixth child of William Turner Prust and Harriet Donkin Walker was Joanna Prust 1816-?

7) Joseph Prust 1818-1818

8) Simeon Prust 1819-1897 Simeon's occupation was a 'Master Butcher' Simeon married twice and had three children Ada Prust 1876, William Prust 1886, and James Prust 1887.

9) Julia Prust, 1821 married George **Welborne** in a double ceremony with her brother John and his bride Elizabeth Pinkney.

10) James Prust 1826-1841

11) Edward Prust 1828-1841.

<u>This concludes the Prust families of Yorkshire.</u>

The Prust Families of Pembrokeshire Wales

17th Century

It is not known what year this Prust family came from Devon to Haverfordwest in **Pembrokeshire,** Wales, but it must have been before the year **1640**. This branch of the Prust family would have been very wealthy.

Robert Prust is the earliest Prust found in Haverfordwest. He was born in about 1640. Robert was Sheriff in 1668 and Mayor of Haverfordwest in the years 1673 and 1683.

Anecdote about Robert Prust: During the Cromwellian struggle, the Town suffered from the levies and exactions of both sides owing to its shifty tactics. Now the Cavaliers would make it pay for its disloyalty to the amount of £160 and cause the municipality to keep the walls and gates of Town and Castle in repair, and then Cromwell would order the demolition of the stronghold. The Rev. James Phillips, in his "History of Pembrokeshire" says, "*On Sunday July 16th (1648)* ***Cromwell*** *rode up to Haverfordwest where he was welcomed with merry peals from the bells of St. Mary's. During his brief stay he was the guest of the* ***Prust family****, at their house near St. Martin's Church, the site of which is still known as 'The Cromwell Corner' Each morning little Bobby Prust the son of his host took him to Gwyn's Ditch or Queen's Ditch off (1) Cokey Street, that he might have his morning draught of the delicious spring water.*

(1) Cokey Street or Cuckoo Street appears to have been what is now called City Road.
Source: "Haverfordwest-Oliver Cromwell July 16, 1648".

The ruins of the Castle at Haverfordwest, Pembrokeshire, still stand today. Shown here on the left.

It is documented that Robert Prust married Elizabeth Thomas on 9 November 1652, and they had ten children together as follows: -

1) Elizabeth Prust, 1653. 3) Thomas Prust 1659
2) Margaret Prust 1657 4) Peter Prust 1661
5) Joseph Prust 1663 6) Stephen Prust 1665
7) Benjamin Prust 1668 8) Thomas Prust 1670
9) Michael Prust 1672 10) Rowland Prust 1677.

In the civil war between the Cromwellian side of the army and the Kings Cavalier forces, most of the Prust family, especially those Prust's from Devon, were on the side of the King, but this branch was not; perhaps they knew 'what side their bread was buttered.'

DEVON TO SWANSEA, WALES, 19th century

This is another branch of the Prust family which moved from Hartland in Devon to Wales. Two brothers, **William Prust** and **Richard Prust** were both born in Hartland in Devon in about **1804**. William and his brother came to **Swansea** in Wales to live and work. William became a maritime pilot, and Richard became a master mariner and shipbuilder. They were both the sons of Thomas Prust in 1772 and his second wife '**Mary Medland** 'of Hartland.

William Prust 1805-1887 with his Irish wife, who was **Catherine Johnson Stuart**. She was born in 1809. They had seven children together, as follows: -:

1) Catherine Johnson Stuart Prust, 1834-1918, she married Richard Randell, and they had two children.

2) **William Medland Prust 1840-1911**, Occupation: Licensed Pilot, married **Rachel Griffiths,** and they had six children.

3) **John Lewis Prust 1841-1911,** occupation: Mariner and Coast Guard. Married **Emma Raven** 1839-1925, and they had three children Herbert John Prust, Frederick William Prust, and William Raven Prust.

4) **Richard Prust 1842-1880**, Occupation: Shipwright/Merchant Navy. Married **Elizabeth Pyke.** They had five children. He died at Sea aged 38 years of a Heart Attack.

5) **Mary Ann Prust, 1845-1918**, married **William Driscoll**. They had no issues.

6) **Martha J Prust 1849-** . she married twice, **John Webb,** with whom she had one child and **Frances Hayes**, with whom she had two children.

7) Isabella J Prust 1856-1920.

The following was from a newspaper article of **1863**

'SWANSEA' *The barque The Duke of Northumberland, of London, had just arrived in Swansea Bay with a cargo of copper ore from Cuba when she anchored in the roadstead at Mumbles to await a berth at the Cobre Mining Company wharf. Late on the afternoon of Wednesday 2nd of December the storm parted her cables, and she was driven across the bay to strand on a sandbank about a mile off Swansea east pier. That evening the Swansea lifeboats named 'Martha' and 'Anne' was launched from the South Dock and stood by the vessel until dawn when she took off the eighteen crew and passengers. At first it was thought that the barque would become a wreck as three steam tugs failed to re-float her. Much of her cargo lighters were then discharged, using lighters she got off the bank and into harbour on 22nd December.*

Another article quoted was that: *On the 2nd of December Edwin Peachey and three other Mumbles men were out in a boat attempting to recover a lost oyster dredge by "creeping" a grappling over the seabed when the storm struck. Luckily their plight was seen by the crew of the pilot boat 'Swanzey' who rescued them and took them into Swansea. The crew of the pilot boat were John Wilkins and James George, both pilots, and assistants Richard Elkington and* ***William Prust****.*

(In those days, the lifeboats were stored under the cliff as there was no boathouse, but one was eventually built in 1865.

William Prust, the pilot, died in Swansea in **1887**.

The boathouse and slipway shown here above was erected in **1922**

The other brother Richard Prust is as follows:
Richard Prust 1808-1884 he married **Jane Davies** in Welcome, Devon and later moved to Swansea in Wales, where all their five children were born as follows:

1) **Mary Jane Prust 1836-1918**, School Mistress, died a spinster and left her money to Richard Prust (Chemist) and William Hopkin-James, Secretary.

2) **John Prust 1838-1881**, John Prust, Occupation: Shipbroker, married **Martha Lloyd**; they had five children. In 1881 John died aged 43 years old at 20, Euston Square, London, in a hotel he owned there. He left his wife Martha £991.1s.10d. Martha Lloyd was, according to the census living with her five children at her father-in-law Richard Prust's house in 1881.

3) **Thomas Prust 1842-1888**, Occupation: Master Mariner, married **Mary Walters,** and they had three children. Thomas was away at sea working on the merchant ship 'Arago' when he died in New Zealand and was buried there aged 46 years old.

4) **Richard Prust 1843-1920**, Occupation: Chemist. Married **Mary Ann Cavill.** They had no children.

5) **William Henry Prust 1845-1915**, Occupation: Shipbrokers Agent and Proprietor of 'The Adelphi Hotel' in London. He married **Evangeline Davies,** and they had six children.

Among his six children, there was **William Aubrey Davies Prust**, who was a Captain in H.M. Army; he was the gentleman who Commissioned 'The Prust Book' in 1912. Refer to page 28.

This concludes the families of the two brothers that settled in Wales.

Prust Family of Westleigh, Devon

This is a 19th-century image of Westleigh village in Devon

This line of Prust families originally came from Westleigh in Devon and, before that, Hartland in North Devon. The generations of this branch of the family had known much poverty and much wealth.

Starting with **William Prust 1789-1878** (Labourer) and **Grace Stevens 1791-1863.** William had the occupation as an Agriculture Labourer.

They had six children: Robert William Prust, William Stevens Prust, John Prust, Mary Prust, Thomas Prust and Joseph Prust. All their children were born in Westleigh, Devon. Their eldest son was:

Robert William Prust 1816-1867. Was born in Westleigh, Devon. But he later moved further northeast to the city of Cheltenham in Gloucestershire, where he made his home. This is where he met and married Miss **Francis Curtis** in **1839,** and together they had eight children. According to records, his occupation was a Painter & decorator. In **1851** according to the census records, Robert was a visitor to his brother's home William Stevens Prust who lived in St. Marylebone in London. Robert and Francis (known as Fanny) had eight children together, Hede Prust, Ester Prust, Mary Prust, Charles Robert Prust, William Prust, Joseph Prust, John Prust and Henry Prust.

The eldest son **Charles Robert Prust** 1846-1900 lived in Bath Street, Cheltenham and had his own business as a Plumber and Glazier.

Their second eldest son was called **William Prust,** he was born in **1847-1927** and married **Ellen Addams** in 1871. They later emigrated to Canada. (Continued on page 124 for more about William Prust and his wife, Ellen).

Cheltenham, Gloucestershire.

Above is an image of an old sepia postcard of Cheltenham taken c.1900.

The second son of William Prust (1789-1878) and Grace Stevens was also called William but given his mother's surname as his second Christian name of Stevens.

William Steven Prust, **1818-1874.** He married Miss **Elizabeth Waters** in Cheltenham, Gloucestershire. His occupation was a Painter, Decorator and Builder like his brother Robert William Prust. In fact, in the year **1851,** William and his brother Robert were together on the 1851 census in Douro Cottage, St. Marylebone, in London. William was self-employed, employing four men together with his brother and son Walter in the family business. The business was doing well until around **1861,** when sadly, William had to file for bankruptcy, like many other businesses around at that time. In 1861 an act of parliament abolished the distinction between Traders and Non-Traders who needed to file for Bankruptcy, making it easier to file. From being a comfortable-off family, they fell on hard times. William

Stephen Prust died in **1874.** William Stevens Prust and his wife Elizabeth Waters had six children:

1) **William Stephen Prust** 2nd **1840-1894**. A Painter by trade. Married to **Elizabeth Hudson**. They had ten children, five of whom were born before the couple married. The family lived in Kensington in London. In the year **1879,** three of their children were sent to Australia under the child migration act in England. The following ten children were:

a) **James William Hudson** born in 1868

b) **Joseph William Hudson** Prust 1868-

c) **Ester Stephens Hudson Prust** 1870-1900 (sent to Australia)

d) **David Prust** 1872-1919

e) **Elizabeth Prust** 1874- (sent to Australia)

f) **Grace Prust** 1876-1880

g) **Moses/Arthur Prust** 1878-1950 (sent to Australia)

h) **Mary Prust** 1881-

i) **Lydia Prust** 1883- and j) John Prust 1887-1908

The Child Migration Act

The government at the time set up the Child Migration Act, a cruel act where families were torn apart, and children were sometimes sent away against their will. This Act involved children who were in foster care or from families that were struggling to cope with being taken from their families and sent to Australia. The children were aged 3-14 years old and invariably were from deprived backgrounds or in some form of social care. There were institutions like the Dr Barnardo's Homes, The Fairbridge Society, and Anglican churches that chose some of these children and helped to organise their emigration. It is not known why these three children were plucked from their families and sent away.

More about the three children that were taken who were –

Ester Stephens Hudson Prust (c) 1870-1900, Ester was born before her parents' marriage and later adopted the surname of 'Prust'. Ester was 17 years old according to her birth certificate, but on the ships manifest, her age is put at 14 years old, maybe she went to look after her sister and brother, so she altered her age! Ester married James Delaney in Hawthorn, Victoria, when she was 29 years old but died one year later aged 30 years.

Elizabeth Prust (e) was born in **1874**, the same year as her parent's marriage. When she was 13 years old, she arrived in Australia. She later married twice, first to Francis J Hoffman and then to Arthur Kimber. Her father is stated as William Steven Prust from England on both her marriage certificates.

Moses Prust (g) was born in **1878**, and he was only nine years old at the time when he arrived in Australia. It is reported that most of these children were brought up in orphanages and children's homes or used as child slave labour when they arrived in **Australia**. They all settled in Hawthorne, Victoria. Through searching ship records, it was found that all three children arrived on the ship 'ABERDEEN' from London. Moses, while in Australia, changed his name to **Arthur Prust** or had his name changed for him. He later married **Elizabeth Christie** and stated on his marriage certificate that his parents were Elizabeth and William Prust from England. Arthur Prust had a family, and he's grandchildren still live in Victoria, Australia, today. Arthur Prust died aged 72 years in **1950.**

The other children of William Stevens Prust and his wife, Elizabeth Waters, are:

1) Emily Bertha Prust 1845- 1875. In 1851 seven-year-old Emily was staying with a relative, a widow called Catherine Prust and Catherine's two servants. One year later, her parents had another child, a boy and the family moved to Marylebone in London. Emily married a gentleman called **Nicolas De Verstoosky,** a diplomat from Finland, and they had three daughters called Tatiana, Catherine, and Florence Verstoosky. In 1871 Emily was living at 9 Gordon Villas, Mansfield Court in Marylebone, London, with her mother, Elizabeth and her three daughters. She stated she was a Gentleman's wife. Her husband was not on the census, maybe out of the country at the time. Sadly, she died in 1875, being only 30 years old. It is not known what happened to her three daughters.

3) Charles Prust 1846-1900

4) James Prust 1850-

5) Walter William 1850-

6) Christopher Arthur Prust 1852-1882, he married **Louisa Ruffley** in Birmingham, Warwickshire and later moved to the parish of Islington in North London. They had two daughters.

1881 Christopher had the occupation of a Vaccination Officer working for The Government, and on his marriage certificate, it states that he is a 'Clerk'.

Both his two daughters married well. The family moved back to Cheltenham, where the girls attended Cheltenham Ladies College

Above is a photograph of Cheltenham Ladies College

Their two daughters were:

a) **Emily Elizabeth A Prust,** who was born in **1878**. Like her cousin Emily Bertha Prust, she also married a man from Finland who she was probably introduced to, a doctor from **Finland** whose name was **Eugene Theodore Edward Conrad De Rossi**. According to the wedding certificate, his father had the profession of a Barrister.

b) **Lillian Bertha Dora Prust** was born in **1880,** and on her birth certificate, her father, Christopher Arthur Prust, stated that he was a 'Gentleman'.

There are some interesting facts about Lillian Bertha Dora Prust. In 1902 in Gloucestershire, she met and married a Nobleman from Russia called **Sergei Alexandroritch Borovikorsky**. His occupation was a Minister of Finance in the Russian government; he was the son of Senator Alexandroritch Borovikorsky.

129

Certificate of Marriage.

1902. Marriage Solemnized at The Parish Church in the Parish of Prestbury in the County of Gloucester

No.	When Married.	Name and Surname.	Age.	Condition.	Rank or Profession.	Residence at the Time of Marriage.	Father's Name and Surname.	Rank or Profession of Father.
35	June 12th 1902	Sergei Alexandrovitch Borovikorsky	31	Bachelor	Noble Ministry of Finance	Liofka 11 S Peters burgh Russia	Alexander Lvovitch Borovikorsky	Senator
		Lilian Bertha Dora Prust	21	Spinster		Post Office Prestbury	Christopher Arthur Prust	Civil Servant

Married in the Parish Church according to the Rites and Ceremonies of the Established Church after banns By me, Henry [illegible] Smith. Vicar.

This Marriage was solemnized between us, Sergei Alexandrovitch Borovikorsky. Lilian Bertha Dora Prust

In the presence of us, S. B. Kitchens Catherine de Rivelietty

The above is a true Copy of the Marriage Register of the Parish of Prestbury aforesaid, the said Register being legally in my custody.

Extracted this Twelfth day of June in the Year of our Lord One Thousand Nine Hundred & Two

By me, Henry [illegible] Vicar of Prestbury

Above is the marriage certificate of Lilian Bertha Prust and her Russian husband

In 1904 Lillian had a son by this marriage, also called Sergei Borovikorsky.

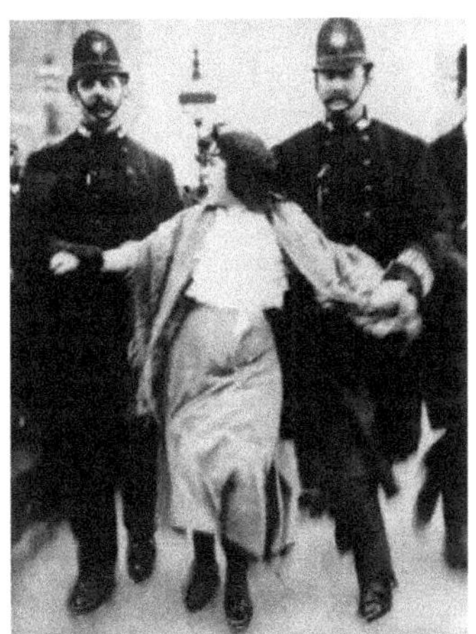

Lily the Suffragette

Although married with a child, Lilian later became a suffragette fighting for women's rights to vote. This is what is known and written about her.

'Lilian Borovikovsky, known as Lilly, was arrested on February 19th, 1909. She was born Lilian Bertha Dora Prust on August 30th, 1880, to Christopher and Louisa. Her father, a vaccination officer, died in 1882, leaving her widowed mother with two daughters aged one and three. Louisa remarried in 1902 with Charles Teague, a Cheltenham musician

who played the organ at the local family church and was a well-renowned cellist. Lilian's sister Emily married and moved to Finland, although she returned to live in Cheltenham in the early 1920s. Lilian married Sergei Alexandrovich Borovikovsky in June 1902; the groom was described as of the Russian Finance Office in Petersburg. Lilian met Sergei through her cousin Helen who was first married to a Russian called Chrouschoff. Just prior to the ceremony, Lilian was baptised into the Church of England. The ceremony was followed by a Russian service at the Russian Embassy in London. Two years later, Lilian gave birth to a son Sergei. In 1905 her husband was appointed to a commission on press censoring by the Czar; embroiled in the Russian crisis, it appears that Lilian returned to Cheltenham to give birth to her son and never returned.

Before she left her husband, Sergei gave her a rare book with a dedication on the front of the book:

Lilian Borovikovsky, St. Petersberg 1906 from Sergei'

(This is written very faintly at the top of the book)

The top title of this book translates to *'From Ukrainian Ancient Time'*, and the bottom line was entitled 'La Petite Russie d Autrefois', which translates to: 'The little Russia of old'. This book shown here was recently found in a rare book sale. As a child, Lilian appears to have attended Cheltenham Ladies College and attended their annual reunions. She became a member of the Women's Freedom League and was elected to the committee in January 1909 at a meeting held at the Cheltenham Vegetarian Hotel. Lilian was part of a delegation led by Charlotte Despard, who attempted to deliver a petition to the Houses of Parliament. They were met by a considerable police presence, including some on horseback. She was arrested and charged with obstruction. Found guilty, she was sentenced to one month's imprisonment, of which she served two weeks as she was released due to failing health. After her release, the Women's Freedom League hosted a reception to welcome her home themed as an American Tea Party and sale. Lilian was clear that she would be more than happy to take part in another demonstration as she now felt more "suffragettish", on this basis, she encouraged all at the gathering to accompany her next time. Lilian was presented with the Holloway badge given to all women who served time in the prison and a copy of the Awakening of Women by Mrs Swiney. All the proceeds were donated to the Despard Prisoners Fund. Lilian continued to be involved with the Women's Freedom League becoming the

Cheltenham Branch Honorary Secretary. During the First World War, Lilian trained with the Red Cross. She was a brave and courageous woman who fought for the rights of women and helped in the war effort. Sadly, Lilian died on May 25th, 1926, aged just 45 years old, as a patient at the Gloucester Mental Hospital Asylum'.

William Prust 1847-1927
and Ellen Addams 1846-1927

(Continued from page 117).

William Prust, the second son of Robert Wm. Prust and Francis Mary Curtis This is a portrait of the couple shown here. William Prust married Ellen Addams in **1871** in Cheltenham, Gloucestershire. William and Ellen immigrated to Canada to make a better life for themselves and their family, so they braved the long journey by sea to start a new life together with their young daughter Ada and eventually settled in the city of Ontario, in Canada, in **1873**. This is where they raised all their five children. William's trade was a carpenter, and he soon found work with these skills. He had various other jobs along the way, but eventually, he set up and ran his own business as a contractor and real estate developer. He built many houses in the town of Haliburton in Ontario.

There was a street sign named after him called 'Prust Avenue': shown here; by the kind permission of his great-granddaughter Debra Prust Kingdon.
William and Ellen had two sons and three daughters.

1) **Ada Emily Prust** was born in **1872-1959.** Ada remained a spinster and died aged 87 years.

2) **Robert Prust** was born in **1874-1954,** aged 80 years. More about Robert Prust on page 127.

3) **Francis Mary Prust** was born in **1879-1970** and died unmarried at age 91 years.

4) **William Ewart Gladstone Prust,** born in **1882-1947,** was no doubt named after The Right Honourable William Ewart Gladstone M.P., the Liberal Statesman and British Prime Minister of that time in England. He married Eva May Jane Evans.

5) **Ellen Faustina Prust** was born in **1885-1951,** aged 66 years.

This branch of Prust of Cheltenham families can be traced back to Benjamin Prust in the year **1666** to Hartland in North Devon.

Robert Prust 1874-1954

This is an interesting story about the life of Robert Prust, the second child of William & Ellen Addams. Robert Prust is pictured here as a cheeky boy of about ten years old.

He was known by the nickname "**Wild Robert**". This is what is known of some of his exploits. He was born in **1874** in Toronto, Canada, the eldest son of William & Ellen Prust. Robert often got into scrapes and trouble when he was a boy. When he was older, he was determined that he wanted adventure and to see the world. To enable him to do this, he signed up for the Navy. He spent his years as a young man working as an 'Able Bodied Seaman' on various boats, travelling all over the world, but most of his time was spent in Australia. When the first World War broke out in **1914,** men from all over Australia began to enlist. This advert was shown as a trumpet call for the calling up of their young men.

In March **1915,** although he was aged 41 years old, he enlisted in The Australian Military Forces and was appointed to Base Infantry. (His attestation paper stated that his father was William Prust of 255 Greenwood Avenue, Toronto, his next of kin.) After two weeks in the army, according to his conduct sheet, he was fined £1.10/- for breaking out of bounds and forfeiture of pay for six days. Robert went on to be absent without leave for a total of six times, forfeiting most of his pay. The last time was for a total of 12 days in May 1915; after just two months, Robert was discharged from the army. The reason given was he was 'unlikely to become an efficient soldier, bad character'.

Some five months later, in October 1916, he thought he would give it another try and enter the army again, so

Robert enlisted in the Australian Army once more under a different name. He now called himself **Robert William Price**, and he changed his age to 35 years and nine months. (His attestation papers state that his mother, Ellen Adams of 255 Greenwood Avenue, Toronto was his next of kin). In May 1917, his Commanding officer wrote, "***Absent without leave, attempting to travel by train without a pass***" Later that month, he was found absent without leave twice more. Robert was arrested and held in custody awaiting trial; his total forfeiture was eight days' pay. Army life wasn't for him and being forty-one years old when he enlisted, he was too old to be moulded into army life, having known the freedom of the sea and doing what he wanted. I would guess that there wasn't much else available for him at that time with the war raging in the open seas. His army record crimes are too numerous to mention ranging from being A.W.O.L. and drunkenness. He was found drunk and was absent without leave on active duty in France. This crime had very serious consequences, as he could have been shot. It was at this point that Robert admitted that his real name was Robert Prust and not Robert Price. He was eventually Court Marshalled in August 1918 and found guilty of drunkenness, being in possession of plunder, and being absent without leave.

Robert was sentenced to 6 months with hard labour but was commuted to 90 days. In between these bouts of A.W.O.L., Robert did serve his regiment in France and was wounded in the field at Rouen, Havre and was admitted to hospital with his injuries. He was still awarded the **British War Medal & Victory Medal.** Robert Prust died in 1954 at the age of 80 years. There was no known issue.

Here below is a photograph of the family grave and monument of the Prust family of Toronto, Canada. William died in 1927, and Ellen died in 1936.

This concludes The Prust Families of Westleigh and Cheltenham.

William Prust OF BRISTOL 1781-1845
Jane Escott 1788-1852
The Customs Officer. Of Somerset

William Prust was born in about **1781**. It is not definitely known who his parents were. Among the Prust families around that time, there were many parents who named their sons 'William' and their daughters 'Mary'. As this is my line, this is most perplexing as my DNA points to both a William and a Thomas Prust, who could have been his parents. And on the woman's side, it also points to Ching/Rowe & Galsworthy, who all were married to members of the Prust family.
Nailing it down, I have concluded that it is more than likely to be Thomas Prust, a Mariner of Bristol. Thomas Prust was the owner of a sloop called 'The John'. The address was Avon Street, Bristol. (Source: date 1775 from Sketcher's Bristol directory) Thomas's wife was called Mary, and William Prust and his wife Jane Escott named their first child 'Mary Ann', and he was also a cousin of Stephen Prust of Bristol, the Merchant and ship owner who also resided in Bristol around that time. William had two brothers **Charles Prust** born in **1782,** and **John,** born in **1783,** residents of Bristol. He also had two sisters, **Susan,** born in **1780** and **Mary,** in **1788.**

The Napoleonic War. It is known that both William and his brother John both fought in the Napoleonic wars of the time.
William Prust was in the navy; records show that he was a sailor on the ship called 'The John of Bristol.' The ship was on a trip from Barcelona in Spain, laden with goods when it was struck by a cannonball. The ship survived, and some surviving men were captured and taken to Brest in France. William spent time in a POW camp in Givet, France, which is on the French/Belgium border. William's eventual release came in the year **1812** when Bristolians raised enough money to buy their release and subsequent repatriation
A list of Prisoners from the Port of Bristol confined in Depots in France, October last, 1812, by a gentleman who has been so active in procuring subscriptions for their relief.
LONGWY: George COOPER, John LEE, John JONES, Stephen LEY, William OKE, Joseph SILCOCK, Thomas OSWALD, ***Edward ESCOTT****, Samuel GRAVES, John ROWLES, John RYAN, William SMITH, Francis MINNITT, John SUMMERS. John Pardo KING, William STOREY, William GARDNER.*
GIVET John WOOD, John BROCK, John OWEN, Abraham NICHOLAS, James SULLIVAN, ***William PRUST,*** *Joseph HERANS.*

Likewise, people from other towns and cities have collected ransom money to release their men. (Source: Felix Farley's Bristol journal 2. January 1813.) On the same ship as William was listed one 'Edward Escott' who was repatriated from Longwy in France. Later William Prust was to marry Edward Escott's sister Miss Jane Escott.

On the 18th of December **1814,** just two years after he returned from France, **William Prust** married **Jane Escott. S**he was the daughter of Samuel Escott and Ann Greenslade, both from the town of Dulverton in Somerset, which is on the edge of the Exmoor National Park in Devon. Jane's father, Samuel Escott, had the occupation of a 'Blacksmith'. The couple were married at the Christian parish church of St. Philip and St. Jacobs in the city of Bristol. They both signed the register, concluding that they were both literate. The witnesses were Janet Davis and Hannah Greenslade Escott (sister of the bride). This parish church is commonly known as Pip 'n' Jay and historically called the 'Mother Church of East Bristol'.

This is the house that William and Jane Prust lived in together with their family at Ashley Road in the parish of St. Philip & St. Jacob Bristol. It is remarkably one of the few houses still standing to this day. I was fortunate enough to be allowed a tour of this magnificent house by the present owner. These houses are extremely spacious, with many rooms, magnificent staircases, original architectural features, and stained-glass windows with servant's quarters at the top. The basement at the back of the property has a courtyard, with an attached coach House built onto the side of it. In the year **1840,** William Prust had the occupation (according to his daughter's marriage certificate) of a 'Gentleman'. The **1841** census, however, gives his occupation as a 'Customs House Officer'.

According to the **1841** census, also living in the Ashley Road area at that time (maybe even in the same house) was a spinster called **Mary Prust**. She was born in about **1761**, presumable an aunt of William Prust but most definitely a relative. Living at Mary's house was her niece Elizabeth Earl nee Prust with her husband. Elizabeth Prust married James Earl by banns in Bristol (register of marriages 1800-1837), her husband James Earl, who had the occupation of a carpenter, together with their young daughter Emma Earl. According to the census Mary who was 80 years old at the time, was of independent means with two live in-house servants. In the December of 1841, Mary Prust passed away, and according to her will, she had changed it in favour of her niece Elizabeth Prust (it is not known what her earlier will said) with the proviso that it was for her sole use only. I found the Earl family ten years later, in 1851, living in **Shoreditch** in East London.

John Prust 1783-1855, William's brother, also fought in the Napoleonic war. It is not known when John joined the Army, but records show his rank was of a private, later promoted in **1812** to corporal in the same year as he married Miss **Jane Slater** in Bristol. John was in the Royal Train Regiment, shown here. The train was heavily involved in the peninsular war, shepherding the wounded and transporting supplies for the British forces, and in the retreat of Corunda, which ended in a triumphant battle against the Napoleonic forces. In June **1815,** eight companies from the Royal Wagon Train were involved. Allied British and Prussian troops faced Napoleon's army at the battle of Waterloo. Victory at Waterloo brought an end to the Napoleonic War. It is quoted that the Royal Wagon Train is one of the unsung heroes of the Napoleonic wars. Shown here are the Royal Wagon Train Regiment WT Ceremonial and Sabretaches. John Prust and his wife Jane Slater had one child called Mary-Ann Prust. John later worked as a mechanic. He died in 1855, aged 72 years old, in Bream, Gloucestershire.

The children of William Prust and Jane Escott, his wife, are as follows:

1) **William Thomas Prust,** baptised on 7 January **1816-1848**. (More about him, refer to page 152)

2) Mary Ann Prust, baptised on 13 September **1818-1893.** More about her, refer to page 136

3) Jane Prust, baptised 10 March **1822-1894,** Twin. More about her, refer to page 139

4) Stephen Prust, baptised 10 March **1822-1903**, Twin. More about him, refer to page 142

5) Caroline Prust, baptised 16 May **1824-1876**. More about her, refer to page 145

6) Charlotte Prust, baptised on 14 September **1828-1828,** died in infancy.

Bristol 19TH Century

Bristol was then a fast-growing industrial town in the 19th century. However, in **1830** although the population was 104,000, only 6000 people were allowed to vote. A bill of reform was introduced by the prime minister of the time 'Lord Grey' in the House of Commons but was later defeated in The House of Lords. When the people heard the news, rioting broke out again in several cities, including Bristol.

In **1831 The Queen Square Riots** occurred, whereupon the mayor of the town of Bristol requested assistance, and a troop of the 3rd Dragoon Guards and a Squadron of the 14th Light Dragoons were sent to Bristol to suppress the uprising. The Dragoon Guards were sent in to violently suppress the rioters of Bristol. The dragoons attacked the crowd, and hundreds of people were killed and severely injured.

By **1831** William Prust was a family man, his eldest son William Thomas would have been about 15 years old, and his youngest daughter Caroline would have been only seven years old; this occurrence must have been terrifying for the young family.

The rioters numbering 500-600 young men, went rampaging through the streets of Bristol for three days, burning down the Bristol Customs house in Queen Street and even entering people's homes where the property was looted and destroyed. Work on the Clifton Suspension Bridge was halted, and Isambard Kingdon Brunel, pictured here, was sworn in as a special constable, which is not widely known. The famous French lady 'Madam Tussaud's' had her travelling exhibition of waxworks near the assembly rooms, and with two-thirds of the square on fire, she was naturally anxious to escape the anarchy and save her precious waxworks. She later took premises in Baker Street, London, where the famous Madam Tussaud's waxworks still stand.

Bristol Customs House is where William Prust was employed in the later part of his life. It is situated in Queen Square, but after the devastation of the riots in 1831, a new building was built on the same site. This was the same year as a dreadful Cholera outbreak which led many people to their deaths, especially in the city's very first workhouse in Bristol.

1845. William Prust's obituary appears in The Bristol Mercury 20.12.1845. It reads simply, *"Dec 11, deeply regretted, Mr William Prust of Ashley Place."*

According to his death certificate, he died of bronchitis and a congested heart. He was buried at St. Paul's, Portland Square, Bristol. His occupation was given as a former proprietor, according to his death certificate. In **1852** William's widow Jane Prust died, aged 64 years old, at her home in Ashley Road, Bristol, of bronchitis. Her obituary also appears in The Bristol Mercury: *"Mrs Jane Prust, Nov 10, aged 65, of Ashley Road, Bristol"* Her occupation on the death certificate was stated as 'wife of Customs House Officer'. The Informant to her death was her daughter-in-law, Elizabeth Thomas Prust (nee Pascoe), who was herself, by then, a young widow with three small boys.

William and Jane's first child was **William Thomas Prust,** who was born about 1816. He married **Elizabeth Thomas Pascoe**. More about this couple is on page 152.

Mary Ann Prust 1818-1893
Charles Adams Bush 1806-1881.

The second child of William Prust and his wife Jane Escott (Re: page 130) was Mary Ann Prust. She was born in the district of Redcliff in Bristol and was baptised at St. Philip and St. Jacob Church in Bristol. It is now known that Mary Ann Prust was <u>adopted at the age of eight years old.</u> Strangely this fact has been unearthed by the will of a gentleman called **William Lloyd Esquire**, as he names Mary Ann Prust as a beneficiary in that will. This, the last will and testament, was unearthed and transcribed by Chris Keher, a descendant of the Prust/Drew family in Australia. He found that Mary Ann Prust was adopted at the age of 8 years old by this rich elderly gentleman. There is no clue as to why this happened as her parents, as far as research shows, were not of a poor class that needed to adopt their daughter out of the family, but we will never know. Maybe they were well rewarded for allowing this to happen. William Lloyd states in his will that she was his adopted daughter and that she has been living in his household since then. According to the 1841 census, William Lloyd was living in Somerset (Somerset is where Mary Ann's mother, Jane Escott, came from) at the time. William Lloyd was 84 years old, and Mary Ann Prust was 23 years old, according to the census, together with her sister Jane Prust who was probably visiting her sister at that time. Mary Ann Prust had no occupation, but her sister Jane's occupation was of a Dressmaker, so she had to work. William Lloyd was a Barrister of Law and was very wealthy indeed. When William Lloyd died later in the year 1841, he left various large sums of money to various institutions and to his adopted daughter Mary Ann. He left her £3000 in his will, which in today's money is worth about £350,000. One year after the death of her adopted father, Mary Ann Prust married **Charles Adams Bush** on 13 February **1842** in the parish church of St. Paul in Bristol. She was 23 years old, and he was 37 years old. Presumably, William Lloyd arranged for his adopted daughter to marry before he died as Charles Adams Bush was also mentioned in the will of William Lloyd,

leaving him also the sum of £3000. Charles Adams Bush was of Bridlington, in Somerset. He was the son of Samuel Bush, a gentleman. After they married, they purchased a house in The Paragon (as shown on the previous page), which is in the town of Bath. These Georgian houses appeared in many historical dramas on Television today.

On the marriage certificate, Charles Adams Bush gave his occupation as a 'Gentleman', and Mary Ann's sister Jane Prust was one of the witnesses. Charles Adams Bush was also, according to the census records, a 'Physician and a Barrister' He was a well-to-do gentleman of some standing in the community. They went on to have a large family of ten children, employing many servants and a resident governess for their children. Charles Adams Bush died in 1881, aged 75 years old, and Mary Ann Bush died in **1893**, also aged 75 years old. She survived the death of four of her six sons and two of her four daughters. She Left her estate to two of her surviving daughters.

Jane Prust 1822-1894 Joseph Drew 1819-1885

3) Jane Prust was born on 17 February 1822, a twin together with her brother Stephen Prust. She was baptised on the 10 March **1822** in the parish church of St. Philip & Jacob's together with her twin brother Stephen in the parish of Clifton in Bristol. Jane married Joseph Drew of Bermondsey, Surrey, on 15 October **1851** at the parish church of St. Barnabas in Bristol, shown here. He was 29 years old, and Joseph was 32 years old. Previously according to the 1851 census, Joseph Drew was a lodger in the home of Jane's widowed mother, Jane Prust, in Ashley Road, Bristol. Joseph's occupation was a Leather Draper working for his own family business called Drew & Co., Oil & Leather Warehouses in Surrey, England. (It is recorded that the Drew families originally came from the county of Devon) Witnesses to the wedding were Jane's sister and brother-in-law, Mary Ann & Charles Adams Bush, who signed the register. **Immigration:** The Drew family, with their children, travelled to Melbourne, Australia, on the ship 'The Sunshine'. They travelled on an unassisted passage in the year **1857** with their two children, with Jane, who was pregnant with her third child at the time, which wasn't ideal for a journey across the sea at those times. The journey was often long and dangerous, and even in calm weather, a sailing ship might take as long as four months to arrive, but it is not known how long this journey took. Surprisingly Jane went into labour

on the voyage and gave birth to their third child, a son and named him James Sumner Drew (1856-1909). He was born on the 23 December on board a ship two days before Christmas day. The couple's baby son's second Christian name 'Sumner' was in honour of the captain of the ship. The family eventually arrived in Melbourne, Australia, on 28 January 1857. It must have been a happy reunion for Jane as her sister Caroline Prust Box was already living in Australia, having emigrated four years previously in **1853.** (Caroline, who travelled alone **a**s a single woman to Australia, leaving her children behind, although she later sent for them a few years later in 1855 when she was settled). It must have been exciting for the couple's children as they had their young cousins to greet them when they arrived.

Arriving in Australia, the Drew family settled in the town of Guildford, New South Wales, where they raised their six children.
Thomas Charles Drew, 1852-1932, and George Joseph Drew, 1855-1859, were both born in Bristol, England. The following children were James Sumner Drew 1856-1909, born at sea and born in Australia: Caroline Elizabeth Drew 1859-1862, died aged three years old, Alice Maud Drew 1862-1947, and George Harrington Drew 1865-1856 who died an infant.

Joseph Drew died at Clifton Villa, Guilford, New South Wales, Australia. He was buried at Rookwood Cemetery. The inscription on his gravestone reads *"My Husband born in London 17th June 1819. Died at Clifton Villa, Guilford 1 May 1885"*

In the will of Joseph Drew of 35 Erskine Street, Sydney, N.S.W., dated 30th January 1874, he left all his goods, shares, properties, etcetera, to his wife, Jane Drew. Jane died in **1894,** at age 72 yrs. Her inscription reads, *"Wife of Joseph, born Stokes Croft, Gloucestershire, England 17 Feb 1822. Died at Clifton Villa, Guilford, New South Wales."* Jane died of Influenza & bronchitis and was survived by three of her children, Thomas Charles, James Sumner & Alice Maud Drew. Below is a photograph of Thomas Charles Drew with his family circa 1916.

Left to right: Rose, Thomas Charles, Violet, Victoria & Clifton Drew

In the will of Jane Drew, she left all her freehold property, shares etc., to her beloved daughter Alice Maud Drew who remained a spinster until her death. The descendants of Jane & Joseph Drew still reside in Australia today. Jane Prust came from the parish of '***Clifton***' in Bristol, England, so to keep the name alive, Jane and Joseph named their house ***'Clifton Villa'***, and their grandson was named 'Clifton Drew' Joseph Drew left in his will all his worldly goods to his wife Jane Drew and she, in turn, left all her assets of £1,245 to her daughter Alice Maud Drew which in today's money is worth approximately £173.000 or $355,000 dollars,

End Note: The descendants of Jane & Joseph Drew are **Drew, Shaw** & **Keher** in Australia.

Stephen Prust
The Tailor
1822 - 1903

Martha Sage 1822-1872
Ann Moffet 1823-1894

Stephen Prust (Twin) was baptised on 10 March **1822** in the parish of St. Philip & Jacob in Bristol. The name 'Stephen' was not a common name around at the time, so it could be that he was named in honour of Stephen Prust of Bristol's whose son, sixteen-year-old Stephen Summer Prust, sadly died the previous year at Oxford University in **1821**. There is no doubt that the families knew one another as both Stephen's father, William Prust and Stephen Prust were involved in seafaring occupations in Bristol. However, what relation they had to one another is not sure at this time.

Stephen was born on the 18th of Feb **1822** at Stokes Croft, Bristol, Gloucestershire. He married twice; his first wife was Martha Sage of Taunton in Somerset; they were both 21 years of age at the time. She was the daughter of James Sage of Taunton in Somerset, whose occupation was also a Tailor. Stephen and Martha had eight children, all of whom were educated.

1) **Stephen Alfred Prust**, **1845-1928**. Solicitor's Clerk
2) **Ellen Jane Prust**, **1849-1871,** died aged 22 years
3) **Lavinia Jeanette Prust**, **1851- 1926,** married **John Gooding**
4) **Joseph Edwin Prust**, **1857-1945,** married, no issue.
5) **Henry Albert Prust,** **1859-1863,** died aged four years.
6) **Martha Emily Prust**, **1861-1931,** married **Charles Coard**
7**) Henry Escott Lawson Prust 1865-1950,** immigrated: Aus.
8) **William Thomas Prust** **1867-1943,** brewery Traveller

(Note: the significance of some of the family names being passed down the generation).

The Coming of the Railways

The coming of the Great Western railways in Bristol created great economic and social change. One of the lines went from Temple Mead, Bristol, to Paddington, London. The trains were steam locomotives, and the grand carriages were painted two-tone chocolate and cream for passengers and red for freight. This was the time of the Second Industrial Revolution, also known as the Technological Revolution.

Temple Mead Station in Bristol, designed by the great Isambard Kingdom Brunel, opened in **1840,** but in **1850** a law was passed that most passengers were afforded the luxury of covered carriages. The station was extended in 1852 with a railway ticket office and train shed. The price of a ticket was one penny per mile. The journey from Bristol to London Paddington station was about 120 miles, so the ticket price at third class was ten shillings (50 pence in the currency of today), bearing in mind the average man's wage was just twenty shillings per week so that would be half a week's wages.

In **1851** Stephen, his wife Martha and their three children had moved from Bristol and were living in a large house in Westmoreland Street, Shoreditch, in London's East End. Also living in this house was his sister-in-law Elizabeth Thomas Pascoe's two sisters: Mary Thomas Pascoe and Bethulia Thomas Pascoe, with her husband Edwin Pascoe and their three children (who also later immigrated to Australia).

According to census records of **1861,** Stephen Prust (who was a 'Tailor' by trade) and his family were living together with one servant in Swan Street, Lambeth. Even the middle classes could afford servants in those days! In 1872 Stephen's wife Martha Sage died aged 50 years old, leaving Stephen with the youngest child (known as Willie), who was just five years old at the time. One year later, in 1873,

Stephen married again. His second wife was a widow called **Ann Moffett,** who was also a Tailor by trade and was no doubt an immense benefit to his tailoring business as well as caring for the youngest children. She died in 1894. Stephen Prust died in **1903**.

Henry Escott Lawson Prust 1865-1950 (known as Charles)

He was the seventh child of Stephen Prust and Martha Sage, and out of all the children, I found his life the most interesting.

Henry immigrated to Australia like his two aunts, Jane and Caroline.

Later Henry married the descendant of a Convict called 'Edith Strange' who was from Christchurch in New Zealand. The family lived in Victoria, and they had one daughter called **Ione Beale Prust,** who married John Gilbert Buckley Castieau in **1915.** John Gilbert Castieau's occupation was a lawyer, and he had the prodigious title of The Assistant **Attorney General of Australia.** This is according to Who's Who in Australia: *Married Ione Beale Prust the daughter of Henry Escott Lawson Prust.* Henry's hobbies are quoted as Golf and Gardening.

Ione and John Castieau had no issue, as although Ione gave birth to a son, shortly afterwards, the baby sadly died.

John Buckley Castieau, the father-in-law of Ione Beale Prust, was the governor of Melbourne Gaol that hung the infamous highwayman Ned Kelly! Here is a drawing by John Castieau's son Geoffrey Castieau showing the trial of Ned Kelly with John Castieau at the back and in the forefront (bearded) Ned Kelly.

Caroline Prust 1824-1876 John Player Box 1820-1844 William Attkins 1820-

This story is about a young lady who was born in the early part of the 19th century in the city of Bristol. Her name was **Caroline Prust;** she was baptised on 16 May **1824** in the parish church of St. Philip & St. Jacob. She was the 5th child of William Prust, a Customs Officer and his wife, Jane Escott. Caroline was educated by her mother, so she was literate in reading and writing, which wasn't the norm for young women of the time. She was a pretty and spirited young girl, which sometimes didn't go down too well with her parents. In 1831 when Caroline was seven years old, riots broke out in her hometown of Bristol. The rioters burned down The Bristol Customs House in Queen Street (this is where her father worked as a customs officer) before going on the rampage through the city. Work on the famous Clifton Suspension Bridge was halted, and the engineer Isambard Kingdon Brunel was sworn in as a special constable. The Mayor of Bristol requested assistance, so a troop of Dragoon guards were sent to Bristol to suppress the uprising. The dragoons attacked the crowd, and hundreds of people were killed, and many more were severely injured. So even at seven years old, Caroline must have learnt that life was sometimes cruel and, on occasion, violent and death was a matter of common fact and could be just around the corner.
In 1838 fourteen-year-old Caroline Prust was entered down as an informant of the birth certificate of her nephew as she was present at the birth of William Henry Prust, the son of her brother William and sister-in-law Elizabeth Pascoe Prust.

In or before **1840,** Caroline fell in love with a dashing 20-year-old man who was lodging at her parents' house in Ashley Road whilst working in the city of Bristol as an accountant. His name was John Player Box, Caroline married John the same year, although the certificate states she was of full age; she was, in fact, 16 years old, and John was only 20 years old.

Page 26.

1840. Marriage solemnized in the Parish Church in the Parish of Horfield in the County of Gloucester

No.	When Married.	Name and Surname.	Age.	Condition.	Rank or Profession.	Residence at the Time of Marriage.	Father's Name and Surname.	Rank or Profession of Father.
45	July 11th	John Player Box Caroline Prust	full age full age	Bachelor Spinster	Accountant	Horfield Horfield	Charles Player Box William Prust	mariner gentleman

Married in the Parish Church according to the Rites and Ceremonies of the Established Church by me, H. G. Richards

This Marriage was solemnized between us, John Player Box, Caroline Prust; in the Presence of us, Jane Prust, John Stallard

According to the 1841 census, Caroline and John Player Box were living with her parents in Ashley Road Bristol, although they were not entered down as a married couple as he was listed as a lodger. His occupation was given as an accountant.

In July of 1841, Caroline gave birth to a son called **Theodore William Augustus Prust Box.** This grand-sounding name was probably to please both sets of grandparents. The following year in June of 1843, Caroline and John had another son, and they called him **Charles Adolphus Box.**

1844 Tragedy struck when Caroline's husband died of Consumption; he was just short of his 24th birthday. He died at Queen Square with his father in attendance. See the death certificate above.

Caroline must have been completely devastated at the time as not only did she have two young sons to bring up, but she was also two months pregnant at the time. In April **1845,** Caroline gave birth to twins, a son and a daughter. The son was named John Player Box after his father, and the girl was named Susanna Jane Box after her mother-in-law Susanna and her mother, Jane. Caroline was by now only 20 years old and a widow with no prospects but relying on the charity of both her parents and in-laws for help with her children.

In **1845** her father, William Prust, died at the family home in Ashley Road, Bristol and in **1847,** another blow struck as her daughter, two-year-old Susanna, became sick and sadly died.

Four years later, in **1851,** Caroline was living with her father-in-law Charles Box with her youngest son John Player Box in his family home in Queen Street, Bristol. Her second son Charles Adolphus Box was a boarder at a school in Bristol, and the eldest child Theodore William Augustus Prust Box was living with her widowed mother, Jane Prust. That year also brought the tragic news that her brother William Thomas Prust had met with an accident and died in London whilst on business, leaving his wife and her sister-in-law Elizabeth Pascoe Prust also a widow with three young children, the youngest being only two years old. These two ladies had a lot in common, both widowed young with young children to bring up. The good news that year was that Caroline's sister Jane Prust married Mr. Joseph Drew, who was previously a boarder at her parents' house in Ashley Road, Bristol. The following year, in **1852,** Jane Escott, their mother, fell ill with Bronchitis and died at the family home with her daughter-in-law Elizabeth Pascoe Prust present at her death.

So now the year is **1853.** So what does Caroline decide to do? She Emigrates! Caroline Prust was a brave woman for her time, and so to survive and make a better life for herself and her surviving children, she left her children in the care of relatives and emigrated **to Australia.** Not easy for a 28-year-old woman on her own. Whilst living in Bristol, she heard of passages to be had for as little as one pound through a crew member who was a Chief Engineer and who was due to board a vessel working on an immigrant ship sailing to Australia from Ireland. This ship was 'The Beejapore' sailing from Tipperary in Ireland for the princely price of just one pound to New South Wales in Australia. Thinking of her and her children's future and hearing what life could possibly offer her in 'The New World,' she decided to Emigrate.

This Chief Engineer tells her about the perilous journey, and as a young and attractive single woman, she would attract the unwanted attention of many men on the journey. It was then agreed that if she decided to travel, she should tell everyone that she was engaged to the Chief Engineer.

The Journey on 'The Beejapore'

So, in **1853** 28-year-old Caroline, with very little money and a heavy heart, decided to make the journey alone. According to the ships manifest, she was a single woman travelling under her maiden name of Caroline Prust; she paid £1 for an assisted passage and had given her occupation as a 'Cook'. It also gave her parents' names as Wm & Jane Prust of Bristol. It also said that '***This girl said she is engaged to the Chief Engineer.***

[illegible]	19	[illegible]	[illegible]	[illegible]	[illegible]	[illegible]	[illegible]	[illegible]	[illegible]	[illegible]	[illegible]
Prust Caroline	28	Cook	[illegible]	[illegible]	[illegible]	[illegible]	None	good	[illegible]	Paid £1.	

Bravely she embarked on this dangerous journey across the other side of the world, which would take her 58 days, and on the way, she and her fellow passengers would endure many hardships with much illness and death. Afterwards, this ship was called the Bad Beejapore. It sunk ten years later on a voyage to Peru.

Arrival of the Beejapore at Sydney in February 1853

There is a newspaper article regarding this ship that was said to be overcrowded, stating that this ship was put in quarantine as there was so much sickness in the 58-day voyage as fifty-five people died of Measles and Scarlet Fever, which mainly affected the children. *The ship was quarantined at Spring Cove off Sydney Head and flew the yellow quarantine flag. Some seven days later after the ship docked Caroline was allowed to land. It is stated that some 228 people were buried after the quarantine and the primary reason was Scarlet Fever, Measles and Typhoid Fever. It is said that some 172 unmarried females were lodged at 'Hyde Park Barracks' where they could be employed by employees whose respectability is known to the immigration officer, provided that the employees do not keep inns of public entertainment!*

Caroline met her second husband, **William Attkins,** soon after arriving in Sydney. He was a widower living in Sydney and owned a Boarding House; she later married him in Sydney in **1853,** giving her real name as Caroline Box on the wedding certificate. 2 years later, in **1855,** she sent for her sons to join her in Sydney, Australia. Therefore, Theodore William Augustus Prust Box, Charles Adolphus Box and John Player Box travelled alone but in Saloon first class on the ship 'The Governor General' to make that long journey, eventually to be reunited with their mother. Caroline must have been ecstatic to have her three boys with her once more.

Another tragedy was to befall Caroline, as this excerpt from a newspaper cutting shows, as in **1857**

Caroline's son, John Player Box, died in a tragic accident! This story was recorded in **'The Maitland Mercury & Hunter River General Advertiser' on Tuesday, 13 January 1857.**

MELANCHOLY CASE OF DROWNING*: On Saturday afternoon John Player Box, a boy of about twelve years of age, the stepson of Mr. Attkins, and a general favourite with all who knew him fell into the river near the back of Mr. Bussells premises, and was drowned.*

At about four o'clock in the afternoon, he called at the house of Mrs, Bussell, near the river, and obtained some fresh meat for bait, as he was going to fish. Shortly after he was seen sitting on the steps or logs at the riverbank, with another boy of about his own age, named Alfred Allwood, both fishing. His companion, catching a fish, ran home with it, 'leaving" his line with young Box, and on his return saw him struggling in the water, which almost covered him. He called out for help, and hurried up the bank to tell Mrs, Bussell; but when he went down again with aid all that could be seen was the hat of the deceased floating down the stream.

In a very short time four or five boats were out, and every exertion was made by dragging to recover the body, several persons dived into search; but the muddy state of the water prevented the divers from feeling well, and the quantity of bottles and broken glass at the bottom rendered the task one of some danger.

Towards six o'clock some aborigines arrived and persevered in diving and swimming about under water until the efforts of one of them proved successful. The poor boy still held the rod and line with which he had been angling. The bait was off the hook; and it was thought possible that the jerk of a fish or eel pulling at the line might have dislodged him from his seat, for he had lost a leg some time ago, and would thus be more easily over balanced. An inquest was held in the evening, before Dr McCartney, at the Shamrock Inn, when some of the above facts were elicited. The verdict was accidental death by drowning. "It appears desirable that a proper apparatus for dragging should be procured and placed in some accessible spot, under charge of a suitable person. It would be superfluous to praise those who so readily came forward to assist on such sad occasions, but it is a pity that probability of succour attending their persevering and well-directed efforts should be diminished by the want of appliances".

It is not known how John Player Box lost his leg prior to his death.

This is a newspaper cutting from Wednesday, **17th March 1875,** from the Maitland Mercury as follows: -

Assault: Henry T. Plews was yesterday charged before the bench with having assaulted ***William Atkins****, by striking him with a whip, at East Maitland, on 24th May. The witnesses called were William Atkins, Charles Box, Benjamin Cutler, and James Betteridge. Complainant stated that on 24th May he was at East Maitland, and about six o'clock in the evening was outside Mr. Cobcroft's house with his stepson. Defendant came up and asked his stepson* ***(Charles Box)*** *whose mare he was riding on (alluding to a roan mare) and claimed it as his property. Complainant said the mare was his, and defendant said it was a lie; he then seized hold of the bridle and insisted on bringing the mare down to the bazaar to be inspected by a friend of his.*

Caroline died of bronchitis on the 8th of August **1876** in Sydney, Australia, aged 52 years. On her death certificate, her profession was a 'Boarding Housekeeper', and she lived at 17 Cowper Terrace, Clarence Street, Sydney. Her father was named as 'William Prust' occupation, a Gentleman and her mother were named Jane, and her maiden name was 'Escott'. The informant of her death was her brother-in-law Joseph Drew of 17 Clarence Street, and witnesses were Joseph Drew and James S Drew. Joseph Drew was the husband of her sister Jane.

The surviving children upon her death were Theodore & Charles Box, whose descendants still reside in Australia.

Records show that **Charles Adolphus Box** married a lady originally from Prussia called **Emma Bertha Christiana Beck Beer** in Goolagong, New South Wales, in 1867. They had three daughters. Sadly, Emma, his wife, died aged only 27 years old, leaving three young daughters in 1874. Charles Adolphus Box died five years later, aged 35 years when he was found drowned in the Goulburn River in Victoria, Australia. It is not known who cared for these little girls, but all three married and went on to have a family of their own.

Theodore Box married a lady who emigrated to Australia from Ireland. She was called **Eliza Stanley,** and they had ten children.

Their eldest surviving son was called Joseph Stanley Box, and he started a building company called Box and Co. (Property) Ltd. in Australia. This company is still in business today in Queensland through successive generations

TODAY

Box & Co are proud to continue servicing the Queensland construction industry in keeping with the values and ethics established by J.S. Box & Co Pty Ltd and G & J Box Pty Ltd.

And so, the generations go on.......

Going back to the first child (page 135) of William Prust and his wife Jane Escott was their son: -

William Thomas Prust *& His Wife,*
1811-1889
A Coach body maker

Elizabeth Thomas Pascoe 1816-1848
A Cornish Lady

William Thomas Prust was born about 1816 in Bristol. He was the first child of William Prust and his wife, Jane Escott. William married Elizabeth Thomas Pascoe at the magnificent church of St. Mary Redcliff in Bristol on 27 March 1837.

Elizabeth Thomas Pascoe was the third child of Henry Pascoe and his first wife, Ann Thomas, both of Cornwall. Henry Pascoe had the occupation of a Mineralist and Mineralogist and styled himself as a gentleman. The two witnesses at their wedding were Edward Pascoe (brother of Elizabeth) and Jane Prust (sister of William)

On 17 November 1848, their first child was born at the family home on Ashley Road. Bristol, and they called him **William Henry Prust**. According to his birth certificate, his father's occupation was a coach builder. The informant at his birth was William's sister, 14-year-old Caroline Prust (page 145). He sadly died within a few days of his birth.

Their second child was **William Edward Pascoe-Prust,** (More about him on page 166). He was born on the 14 August **1841**, at Barton Street, Bristol. His mother, Elizabeth, was staying at the family home of the Pascoe family. It is more than likely that Elizabeth spent the last two or three months of her pregnancy at this address as she is present on the 1841 census which was taken in June of that year. Her siblings who lived there were her two sister's Mary and Bethulia

Thomas Pascoe, and her half-siblings, young Lavinia, Sibella, Eliza, and her 9-year-old half-brother Francis James Polkinghorn Pascoe. It would seem to be a very close family, as letters later show.
At that time, her husband, William Thomas Prust, was staying with his parents in Ashley Road, Bristol. Probably, they might have been estranged as later information shows the marriage could be rocky!

A Biography of the Life of ELIZABETH THOMAS PASCOE

Elizabeth was one of eight children; her mother was Ann Thomas (daughter of William and Ann Thomas of St. Hilary in Cornwall), and her father was Henry Pascoe (son and fifth child of John and Jane Pascoe). In **1822,** When Elizabeth was just 12 years old, her mother Ann died in Wales, leaving children ranging from sixteen years to an infant.

A few years later, her father, the widower wealthy 41-year-old Henry, married a 20-year-old girl called Eliza Polkinghorn, who was the youngest child of fourteen children from Cornwall. Henry and Eliza travelled to London and were married by license at St. George's church in Bloomsbury in June **1823.** Henry's occupation at that time was stated as being a mineralogist, metal refiner and 'Gentleman'. It is known that Eliza Henry's second wife was a kind and loving stepmother to Henry's children, and Elizabeth and her four younger siblings grew to love her. Henry and Eliza went on to have six children of their own together. Sadly in **1836,** Eliza passed away at the home of 'The Prust family in Ashley Road, Bristol, whereupon Elizabeth was stated as an informant on her death certificate. The following year in **March 1837,** Elizabeth married **William Thomas Prust** (page 153) (the son of William Prust and Jane Escott) in the magnificent church of St. Mary Redcliff, Bristol. It would not seem to have been such a happy marriage as events tell us. Elizabeth is thought to have left her husband several times during their marriage. William Thomas Prust put this strange advertisement in The Bristol Mercury to tell all that his wife has left him, and (as in those days, husbands were liable for their wife's debts) the following ad was placed.

20th June, 1837.

THIS is to Certify, that my Wife, ELIZABETH THOMAS PRUST, absconded from me on Tuesday last, the 20th instant, and I do hereby caution any person or persons not to let her contract any debt or debts in my name, as I will not discharge any debt or debts she may contract from the date hereof. W. T. PRUST.

And this is her response as six days later she put this advert in the Bristol Mercury.

IN reply to an Advertisement, stating my having absconded from my husband, W. T. PRUST, I have merely to observe, that his brutal treatment, for which he was committed to prison, and his threat to take away my life, induced me to seek shelter under my Father's roof. E. T. PRUST.

Bristol, 26th June, 1837.

There was no information as to whether Elizabeth's husband, William Thomas Prust, was, in fact, committed to prison. This does show that Elizabeth felt that he had assaulted and mistreated her.

Also, this was the year **1837** when Elizabeth's father, Henry Pascoe, who is now 53 years old, married for a third time just six months after the death of his second wife to a young seventeen-year-old girl called Eliza Grainger, which must have sent shock waves through his existing children. Eliza Granger went on to give Henry a further two children, both daughters. Later Eliza and Henry separated, and she was not present when he passed away. Although Henry had sired twenty children, he made sure they were all educated; even the girls were literate, which held them all in good stead.

In **the 1841** census in Gloucester, we find some of the Pascoe family, mainly the daughters of Henry, living in Barton Street, St. Michaels parish in Gloucester. At that time, Henry was visiting family back in Ludgvan in Cornwall with his sister Mary Pascoe. According to the census, they were Sisters: Mary, twenty-five, Bethulia, nineteen, Francis thirteen, Eliza ten, Lavinia eight, and Sibella, five; and there was thirty-year-old Elizabeth Thomas Pascoe, who was expecting her second baby. Meanwhile, her husband, William Thomas Prust, was living with his parents in Ashley Road, Bristol. It looks like the couple were separated at this time, or being pregnant with her second baby, she chose to stay with her family until after the confinement.

In **1845** Elizabeth gave birth to another son, who they called **Frederick Octavius Prust,** at 28 Picton St., in Bristol. More about Frederick O Prust later (page 173).

In **1848** Elizabeth gave birth to yet another son, and he was called **Theophilus Isaiah Prust** more about him on (page 175)

Between the years **1850** and **1855,** there was a shift in the family dynamics, moving away from the city of Bristol towards London's east end. A timeline shows that in **1850** her beloved father, Henry, dies

1850 also shows that Elizabeth's brother-in-law Stephen Prust moved to Shoreditch in London's East end and rented a large house in Westmorland Street, Shoreditch; living there with his second wife and his children also living there was Elizabeth's sister Mary Thomas Pascoe.

They would have travelled by way of The Great Western Railway, the so-called *"God's wonderful railway,"* which opened great social and economic change. One of the lines went from Temple Mead Station in Bristol, which was designed originally by the great Victorian engineer **Isambard Kingdon- Brunnell,** who also designed/built the Clifton Suspension Bridge. Travelling on this railway line in a steam locomotive in grand carriages, which were painted chocolate and cream for passengers and red for freight, must have been an exciting experience, arriving at Paddington Station in London in less than two hours.

The **1851** census shows that Elizabeth is now a widow; It is not known what happened to her husband, William Thomas Prust, as a death record has never been found.

Elizabeth was an extraordinary woman. According to the **1851** census, Elizabeth was a widow aged only 37 years old and engaged as a school Mistress. She was living at 19 & 20 Conduit Street, Bristol and ran a small boarding school, educating children alongside her own three sons.

The eldest child, William, was aged nine years old; Frederick was five years old, and Theo was about three years old.

That year in **1851,** Elizabeth's sister, Bethulia Thomas Pascoe (pictured here), and her family also moved to Westmorland Street in Shoreditch; she was living next door to her brother-in-law Stephen Prust and his family together with her sister Mary Thomas Pascoe, (Bethulia Thomas Pascoe was married to her cousin John Edwin Polkinghorn Pascoe) and they later **immigrated to Australia** in **1855**. Elizabeth must have been incredibly sad knowing she would never see her beloved sister again, but it is known that they did correspond regularly, as letters recently show.

Elizabeth's brother John Thomas Pascoe who had the occupation of a Metal Refiner like his father, was living in the Whitechapel area with his family and his half-sister Sibella Pascoe. So, it shows that the Prust and the Pascoe families were very close.

Records show that visiting London at that time was Elizabeth's half-brother Francis Polkinghorn Pascoe and his young family; they were visiting family friends in the Stepney area. Francis and his friend attended the Great Exhibition at London's wonderful Crystal Palace (shown above), which was a marvel of its day and a creation of 'Prince Albert', the husband of Queen Victoria. The lowest ticket price to enter the great exhibition was only one shilling, consequently bringing in many thousands of ordinary people. Francis P. Pascoe, with his wife and family, later immigrated to Salt Lake City, Utah, America.

So, the year **1851** is very significant. By now, nearly all the family had migrated south to London and settled in the Shoreditch and the Stepney area of the city, probably where work was more readily available.

In **1861** Elizabeth was now 47 years old and living in Finsbury, London (then it was the county of Middlesex). Also living at this address was her son William Edward Pascoe Prust, aged 21, whose occupation was given as an **Engineer**, his wife Laura, aged 20, and her son Edward who was 15 years old. Theo was living with another family down the road.

Pascoe's in France

Edward Pascoe indeed lived in France, leaving his wife Harriet Clark in Bristol in **1842.** In **1846** four years later, French records show that Edward Thomas Pascoe married a lady called Eleornore Celastine Gouellain in Rouen in France bigamously and went on to have another family. Furthermore, his father, Henry Pascoe, not only lived with him at the same address in Paris but was also complicit and consenting to the marriage. Both were described as 'Copper Miners' on the marriage certificate. Edward Pascoe died in **1861** in his Paris apartment. After Edward died, Harriet, his true wife, was able to marry again, and this she did.

Edward's two sisters (Elizabeth Pascoe Prust's half-sisters), Lavinia and Sibilla, also married and lived in France.

Lavinia Getrude Polkinghorn Pascoe married a French widower and furniture maker from Rouen named Hippolyte Francois Leroy. He was 22 years older than Lavinia. The couple had seven children, five dying as infants. Unfortunately, there are no dates available for Lavinia's death.

Sibella Ann Polkinghorn Pascoe (dressmaker) also married in Rouen in 1856 to Michael Felix Gontier, a widower. They had no children. She died in 1876, aged 42, employed as a cuisiniere (cook).

Elizabeth writes from her home in Hackney, London, to her brother Francis Polkinghorn Pascoe in America. These fascinating letters give a glimpse of a family in times gone by; the following is a sad and poignant letter. This letter was written in 1880 by Elizabeth.

My dear Brother and Sister,

I received your kind and welcome letter and was very glad to hear you are all well in health. I hear the Fever is very bad there. I hope none of you have it. I am very unhappy about it. I hope all is well with you all. I long to hear from you to know how you are getting on. Trade is better with you than when I last heard from you. I am very sorry to hear of it. I hope you are getting on all right in business for trade is very bad here. I am afraid we shall have a very hard winter. I cannot see tonight, the snow is coming down so heavy, I never saw it so large in my life. I should have written to you before being so ill and put about I was not able to write to you. My dear, I felt very unhappy about it, I am very ill, I cannot work. I have a letter from my dear sister Bethulia, she sent me one pound, and she will help all she can. I long to see her, I never shall in this world again. I hope we shall all meet in a better one than this one when we shall ever be at rest. I have sent my likeness to her and a lock of my hair, she will weep over it. She said you sent yours to her. She said how much you are like dear father and kissed it.

I have sent you my likeness, it is very much like me, you can look at the likeness and think of me when I am no more. I hope I shall see my dear Brother and Sister once more. How happy I should be to embrace you once more in this world. I have got my dear sister Lavinia's likeness, it is taken on glass, together with her husband's little boy. I would send it to you but it is too large to send to you. You shall have it when you come to London. If I am dead one of my children will give it to you, my dear sister sent it from France to me. I will send the last letter I had from them at the time the war was on in France. William is doing very bad. I am afraid he will be done up if trade does not change, there is no work to be got, I hope trade will change soon, it is very bad in London. He does strive to get on, he has 8 children to work for. Theophilus has 5 children, he works with his brother Frederick, and he has got a little girl 2 months old. He is the only one who can help me, they would all help me if they had in their power. They are all very kind to me. Try and write by return post. I hope you will be able to read it all. With myself sending kind love to you all hoping you're quite well my dears, ever to be your loving sister. Elizabeth.

In **1881** Elizabeth receives the sad news that her youngest son

Theophilus had died of T.B. (consumption) aged just 35 years old

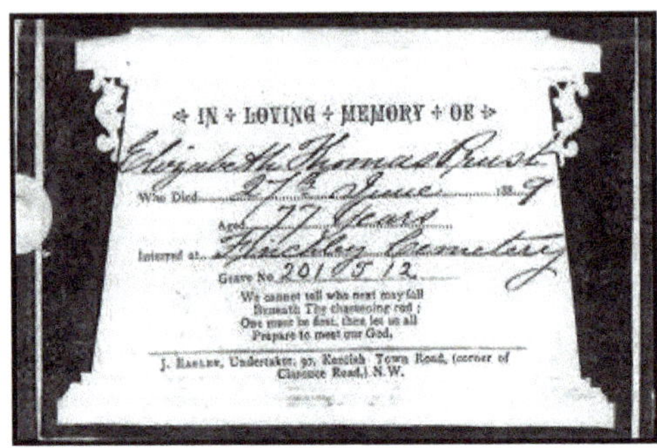

IN LOVING MEMORY OF

Elizabeth Thomas Prust

Who Died 27th June 1889

Aged 77 Years

Interred at Finchley Cemetery

Grave No. 20105 12

We cannot tell who next may fall
Beneath The chastening rod;
One must be first, then let us all
Prepare to meet our God.

J. [illegible], Undertaker, 97, Kentish Town Road, (corner of Clarence Road,) N.W.

The poem on the memoriam card reads:

We cannot tell who next may fall
Beneath they chastening rod.
One must be first, and let us all
Prepare to meet our god.

The following is a letter of interest as it was written by Elizabeth's sister Bethulia Thomas Pascoe when she emigrated to in Australia to her brother in America in **1889,** and it is informing him of the death of their sister Elizabeth Thomas Prust.

This letter on the next page was translated by Carol Fielden, who was a direct descendant of Francis J. Polkinghorn Pascoe. She very kindly sent me copies of the Pascoe papers, which included this letter which I have further transcribed on the following page, which is dated 16th Sept**. 1889**, seven weeks after Elizabeth's death.

Australia. 16 Sept. 1888
My Dear Brother and family,

I received your last letter July 10th and am sorry to hear that you have lost so much in the speculation, but I hope you will succeed in your paint, and that you will be able to form a company for it. I suppose before now you have heard of the death of our dear and only sister. We are but two of us left of the first generation. She

died on the 27th of June after a long and painful illness which she bore with Christian fortitude. May our end be like hers and may we all meet beyond the grave and be able to say to our souls, "It is well with thee it is well"

I am pleased that it was in my power to send her a little money to keep her from want in her old age. It was but little but it repaid me ten- fold for the dear kind letters I received from her in acknowledgment. She was in her 77th year. I am all so sorry to hear of the untimely death of your son. I am glad your health did not give away under such severe affliction. All these troubles are sent for our good, to wean us from the world and to put our trust in one that is mighty to save.

I received the map of Salt Lake City; you have some very fine buildings there. You say you still live in hopes someday of seeing me; I wish that day was come but I think it is a long way off. Give my kind love to my nieces and tell them I should be delighted with their likenesses, and you say you will send the family group. I am anxiously waiting for them.

I have also some bad news to tell you, my daughter is very ill, I am afraid she will never be better, her mind is affected. She had a severe shock to her nervous system, and it has gone to her brain. She took her daughter Edith, her eldest girl about fourteen years and half to a doctor for consultation and the doctor told her she would die, so it went to her brain. The girl is in consumption, I do not think my daughter will live unless a great change, and she has six children. My trouble is almost more than I can bear. You must excuse this scribble as my hand shakes badly. Give my kind love to Maria and hope she is better. I hope you will not be long before you answer this. I remain your affectionate sister in haste.

Bethulia Thomas Pascoe

God bless you all. I hope you will do well in the paint. I forgot to tell you we have some shares in a paint mine in Adelaide, it is just commenced in working order. I think it will be a good thing, I hope so for I want Edwin to have work. We shall not get rich on it but a little to help with the rest. We had a great many shares in different mines but lost all, but not our property.

I thought it appropriate and of historical interest to add a condensed version of the Biography of Elizabeth's beloved brother Francis J. P. Pascoe, with whom the above letter was written.

Francis James Polkinghorn Pascoe'

A Pioneer'

Francis J Polkinghorn Pascoe, shown here, is the brother of Elizabeth and Bethulia Pascoe and their other siblings. He and his wife Eliza converted to the Mormon religion in Shoreditch, East London, in 1860. Soon after, Francis made the decision to go to Salt Lake City, which was the centre of '**The Mormon Religion.'** So, Francis, Eliza and their six children made the long journey across the sea and, from then on, had to travel across the plains of America in a covered wagon which was part of a larger wagon train with a group of other likewise settlers.

They all had the same object in life to get to Salt Lake City and start a new life with their newfound religion. Along the journey, it is known that they encountered hundreds of tribal Indians, which must have been a frightening sight, in all their finery and with their war paint on. They must have breathed a sigh of relief when they found that the war paint was not for them but for another Indian tribe that the Indians were intending to make war on! Nevertheless, the Indians demanded some goods to let them pass on their way peacefully, so the pioneers made a present of flour, bacon, and sugar before they were allowed to go on their way. Eventually, arriving in Salt Lake City in, Utah, America, where Francis bought a house and set up a home with his family. He also started making enquiries straight away about setting up his paint business. He later built a larger house for his family of thirteen children.

Francis had his difficulties and tragedies. One such tragedy was losing his young son 'Lorenzo' in a mining accident in Montana, U.S.A. Francis, with his paint mines, became a very wealthy man. His wife Eliza died in 1891, aged 61 years old, and Francis died intestate in

1903, aged 74 years old. This information came from a short version of his obituary written by his son-in-law Hans W Oblatt.

Information about paint mines: The paint mines are named for their clay deposits which contain iron oxides that colour the clay red, yellow, and purple. This was something Francis knew about being a mineralogist and trained as a Chemist. He also had previous experience in the Cornwall mining industry of the 19th century. Most of the paint in those times contained 'Lead,' but since 1992, Lead paint in the UK has been banned except for specialized use.

Here is an account of what is known of the life of Henry Pascoe (The Father of Elizabeth Thomas Pascoe **Prust**)

Henry Pascoe 1738-1850, Gentleman, Metal Refiner, Mineralist, Mineralogist and Begetter of children.

Henry Pascoe was born in **1783** in St. Hilary in Cornwall, in a small farming community. His parents were John, a 'Tinner', and Jane James, a yeoman's daughter; they married in 1773 and had nine children, the fifth being Henry. In 1803 Twenty-year-old Henry married seventeen-year-old Ann Thomas from St. Hilary, in Cornwall. Henry and Ann went on to have nine children, but only six children survived into adulthood. Henry Pascoe had the occupation of a Gentleman, Metal Refiner, Mineralist and Mineralogist, quite a mouthful! All their children were christened in Ludgvan in Cornwall. The second eldest was Elizabeth Thomas Pascoe, who was born in **1810,** and the youngest was Bethulia Thomas Pascoe, who was born in **1820**. Sadly, soon after the birth of his daughter Bethulia, Henry's wife, Ann Thomas, passed away; she was only 35 years old. In **1823,** forty-one-year-old Henry remarried a lady called Eliza Polkinghorn in St. Georges Church in Bloomsbury, London. She was only twenty years old, less than half of Henry's age. Henry describes himself as a Gentleman, and their address is Queen

Street, London. Henry & Eliza went on to have ten children, but three died in childhood, so there were seven surviving children. The Pascoe's were Wesleyan Methodists, and in June **1836,** his three youngest daughters were christened at Old Market Chapel, Bristol. Lavinia was four, Sibella two, and Lydia six weeks old. Within a matter of weeks, Eliza Polkinghorn, Henry's wife caught scarlet fever and died at the end of July; she was only thirty-three years old. Fifty-one-year-old Henry was now a widow once more and, for the second time, father to a motherless young family. Did his eldest daughters help out? No, his eldest daughter Ann Thomas Pascoe had recently died aged twenty-eight. Did he hire a nurse? What did he do? Well, he got married again!! It wasn't unusual for widowers to remarry, but I find this shocking as not six months after the death of Eliza, Henry married another young girl seventeen years old whose name was Eliza Granger; they married in May **1837,** and Henry and Eliza had two children together.

In **1846** Henry went to stay with his son Edward Thomas Pascoe who lived in Rouen in France, as referred to previously in **Pascoe's in France** page 155. Edward was also a metal refiner like his father. Henry was also a witness and indeed signed the register to the bigamous marriage between his son and a young French lady called Eleonore, knowing full well that Edward already had a wife in their hometown of Bristol. So, he was not, in fact, killed in the Franco-Prussian war as his sister Elizabeth Thomas Pascoe was told and neither were his sisters Livinia and Sibella also settled in France.

Henry and his third wife, Eliza Granger's first daughter, were called Emma Pascoe, but she sadly died aged four years old in **1842.** Their other daughter was called Louisa Pascoe, but she died of smallpox in **1858**. Present at the death of Louisa was a gentleman called 'John Boone' whom Eliza Granger Pascoe later went on to marry after the death of Henry Pascoe, her legal husband. Eliza & John Boone went on to have more children together, so hopefully, a happy ending for Eliza finding love and happiness in the end.

Henry died in **1850,** estranged from his wife Eliza; in fact, at the time of Henry's death, his eldest living daughter Mary Pascoe was with him when he passed away.

Note: Henry Pascoe sired a total of twenty children.

Finally, I must reveal that Henry was a good father – even the girls were literate, and Bethulia writes about "our dear father" In spite of the numbers, it was obviously a close-knit family, especially as there were two marriages between the first cousins.

I will now take the readers through to the London branch of the Prust family, which came from our widow Elizabeth Thomas Pascoe, wife of William Prust of Bristol, who migrated south to Shoreditch and Hackney in London in about 1850. There is more known about this line as it is my direct ancestors, so records and stories still exist.

The London Prust's

William Edward Pascoe Prust **1841-1909 *'The Inventor'***	**Laura Ellis** **1843-1902**

All three sons of William Thomas Prust and his wife, Elizabeth Thomas Pascoe, became Engineers.
The eldest was William Edward Pascoe Prust, who was born in **1841** in Gloucester, but his Christening took place in 1844 when William was nearly three years of age in Bristol.

His father died when he was about eight years old, so life must have been tough for him and his two brothers, with only their mother to bring them up. There were no social services in those days, and if you didn't work, you would starve.
William E.P. Prust married Laura Ellis on April the 1st, 1861. She was the daughter of William Ellis, who was a Coppersmith in London, and her mother's maiden name was Mackay. William was 20 years old, and Laura was 18 years old when they married at 'St. James's Church' in the parish of Shoreditch, East London (then Middlesex). This church was later demolished in 1935. The witnesses at their wedding were William Pascoe (his uncle) and Elizabeth Thomas Pascoe, William's mother. William and his bride Laura moved in with William's mother, Elizabeth, to the family home at 6 Little Galway in Clerkenwell, London, which was near Old Street Underground Station.

In **1862** William, who was by then a working Engineer, and Laura, his wife, moved to a home of their own in Shoreditch, East London. Shortly afterwards, their first child, a daughter, was born, who was named Emily Ann Prust.

1871 Fast forward ten years, and we find the family has increased to five children, and they are now living at 222 Hackney Road in Bethnal Green, East London; also living with the family was Laura's brother Henry Ellis and one domestic servant, so the family was doing well for itself. By then, William's occupation was listed as a 'Master Engineer'. He opened up his own business of engineering works also in Hackney Road, which he named 'Perseverance Works'. The name tells the story of his strive to get on in life and prosper.

Hackney was a good district of London to live and work in, just a few miles from the West End. It was thought to be a cut above the East End of London in the districts of Bethnal Green, Stepney & Poplar. Although it was predominately working to middle class, there were still grand Victorian houses in the area. (William would not recognise the Hackney as it has become today with fashionable shops, restaurants and galleries etc.) By **1874** things were not going so well business-wise, and William on the 20th of May **1874,** William filed for Bankruptcy. The Bankruptcy hearing was held on the 3rd of June 1874, and he was declared bankrupt on the 20th of July 1874 in Lincolns Inn Field in the county of Middlesex. This information was published in 'The London Gazette' in May & June of 1874. Although he was declared Bankrupt, it didn't stop him from trying to better himself, and two years later, with the help of his friend Mr Samuel G Browne, he designed and made an apparatus for the manufacturing industry to be used in the making of boots & shoes.

Here is a copy of his invention which was patented on the 20th of April **1876,** Patent No. 1653, signed and patented by William Edward Prust on the 20th of October 1876

Invention Patented. There are eight pages of specifications and 11 fig. drawings. This is only one fig. 1 of his drawings.

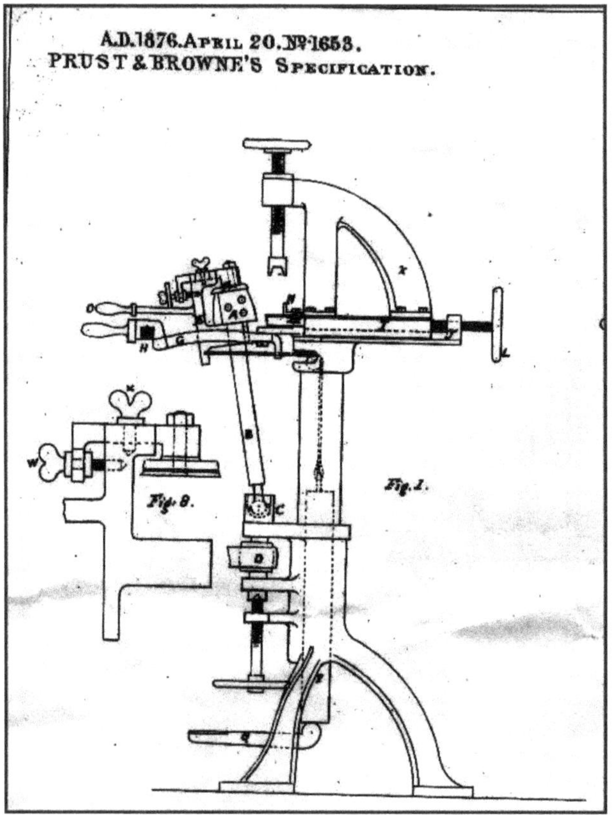

This excerpt was taken from a page of the London Gazette.

"William Edward Prust, of Hackney Road, in the county of Middlesex, and Samuel Graham Browne, of Cavendish-road, Kilburn, in the same county, have given the like notice in respect of the invention of "improvements in the machinery or apparatus to be used in the manufacture of boots and shoes."

It is not known if he made any money from this invention.

In **1880**, times were once again hard in London as an excerpt of this poignant letter shows, written by William's mother Elizabeth Thomas Pascoe Prust to her half-brother in America, Francis J. Polkinghorne Pascoe.

"Trade is very bad here; I am afraid we shall have a very hard winter. I cannot see tonight the snow is coming down so heavy, I never saw it so

large in my life. I am ill, I cannot work. ***William is doing very bad; I am afraid we will be done up if trade doesn't change.*** *There is no work to be got. I hope trade will change soon as he does strive to get on, he has 8 children to work for."*

The year now is **1882,** and William is now forty-one years old with a family of eight children.

1) **Emily Ann Prust, 1882,** married **Hyam Dupare** (a Jewish Jeweller)

2) **Laura Prust, 1866-1884.**

3) **Bethulia Prust, 1864-1907,** married **Frederick John Kirkland**.

4) **William Edward Prust, 1867-1925,** married **Emily Lucy Keeping** (page 176)

5) **Alice Ellis Prust, 1869-1911** (a breach of promise court case in 1894, see page 169). She married **Ernest E Barter**.

6) **David Andrew Mackay Prust, 1872-1936**, David was a Lithographic Artist and married **Louisa M Theobalds**, they settled in Southend on Sea. They had no issues.

7) **Louisa Adelaide Prust, 1879-1952** she married **William Beattie,** and they had two daughters.

8) **Arthur Watson Prust, 1880-1952.** Arthur was an Engineer also but later bought an off-licence premises in Hackney. He remained a bachelor until he died in Hackney with his niece Ethel C.C. Grey in attendance at his death.

This is an interesting story about a court case which was about **Alice Ellis Prust** (the fifth child of William & Laura Prust). This was recorded by The Reynolds Newspaper and illustrated by The Penny Post. Although I was interested in this piece of history, I later found that I had a more personal connection as Alice Ellis Prust was, in fact, my 3rd great Aunt!

This article was taken from the Penny Illustrated Post in 1894

Sketched in Court by a "P.I.P." Artist.

RECORDED BY THE REYNOLDS NEWSPAPER 1894.

Prust v Stephenson

An Infants breach of promise case.

"Miss Alice Prust last week sued in The Queen's Bench before a judge and special jury, in action to recover damages for Breach of Promise of marriage. Miss Alice Prust was the daughter of a working Engineer, **Mr. William E. P Prust** of Sandringham Road, Dalston. The defendant was Mr. Sedley William Stephenson, an Auctioneer and Livery stable keeper of Kentish Town. Mr Bell, on behalf of the young lady, said in court that she and her sister Bethulia were formerly attendants and sellers of programmes at The Grand Theatre in Islington.

The Grand Theatre, Islington, London

Mr. Bell goes on to say that the Plaintiff had no actual salary, but by her commission on the sale of programmes and her tips, she made a nice little income. It was her sister and not Alice who first fascinated the contemptible defendant, but after the three of them went together to Yarmouth on a Bank Holiday, the defendant transferred his affections from one sister to the other and chose Alice.

Mr. Dudley Wm Stephenson, the defendant, said that he never asked the plaintiff to give up her situation at the theatre. He was nineteen years old last birthday. He positively contradicted some of the statements which had been made as to his having requested the plaintiff to give up her situation and as to his age. The plaintiff 'Alice, was called to the stand and stated that the engagement was sealed by a diamond ring, which she chose out of two that he bought, with a request that she should choose the one with the largest diamond in it, but as time went on last year the affection of the defendant cooled! Alice wrote him three letters which he never answered and then she called his office in Kentish town for an explanation, he then said that he could not write love letters, only business ones.

The defendant had told her that he derived ten pounds a week from his business and that he owned house properties in Barnet and Highgate. But the jury, after some consideration, found that the defendant had falsely represented that he was over age and that he did this with the intention to deceive the plaintiff; but she was not induced by the statement to accept his offer of marriage. Mr. Justice Bruce said that upon those findings, he should enter a verdict for the defendant and that the costs must follow this result". Damages were assessed at £150.

The purchasing power in 1894 in today's money is today's equivalent of just over £19,500!

Another Breach of Promise case in the same year, **1894,** is an action brought by a young lady called Anna Lewis, whose occupation was a 'Barmaid'. Miss Lewis sued to recover damages for the Breach of Promise to marry. The defendant was William Sandy, the son of a local farmer in the neighbourhood. Anna, the plaintiff, alleges the defendant gave her an engagement ring and after which he had **immoral relations with her.** After a short deliberation, Anna was awarded £80 in damages. Worth in today's money approximately ten thousand pounds.
In comparative contrast regarding subsequent awards given to women of that year, this was the horrific case regarding servant women, who were regarded as lowly in social status in the nineteenth century. Her name was Margaret O'Toole, and she too was in court to recover damages from Mr J Parkinson, a Dentist of Liverpool who allowed his assistant to place her under chloroform and **remove all her teeth against her will**. Miss O'Toole received £150 damages, the same amount as Miss Alice Prust, for her 'Breach of Promise' action.

Alice Prust later married in Hackney in the year 1900 when she was twenty-one years old to Ernest E Barter, and they had two sons. Alice, Ernest, and their children moved to Southend on Sea in Essex, where she died aged 77 years old in **1925.**

1891-1901 William Prust and his wife Laura were still living in Hackney. Laura Ellis Prust Died in **1902,** and William Edward Pascoe Prust died aged 68 years old in **1909** in Hackney.

Frederick Octavious Prust
1845-1894

Maria Whiter
1857-1939

Engineer & Dental Appliance Maker Machinist

Frederick Octavius Prust was the second surviving son of William Thomas Prust and his wife, Elizabeth Thomas Pascoe Prust. He was born in **1845** at 28 Picton Street in Bristol. In **1878** Frederick, then 33 years old married twenty-year-old Maria Whiter in 'All Saints Church' in Haggerston, East London; his occupation is given as an Engineer. They lived in Shoreditch and later moved to Kentish Town in **1891**. The family's address is 'The Dental Factory', Anglers Lane, Kentish Town, London. They had seven children; three daughters and four sons as follows:

1) Louisa Maria Prust 1879-1890.

2) Florence Elizabeth 1882- 1945.

3) Emily Elizabeth 1884- 1887.

4) Frederick Henry Prust 1888-1973.

4) Frederick Henry Prust, whose photo is shown here, was named after his father but with the second name of Henry, probably after his grandfather Henry Pascoe.

Soon after the outbreak of World War I in 1915, Frederick joined the Australian Army and saw active service in France. He immigrated to

Australia in **1911,** where he met and fell in love with a lady called **Lila Hope Mann** at the amateur dramatic society to which they both belonged, where Fred (as he was known) played the part of 'Marc Anthony' and won the heart of Lila. Frederick and Lila married, and after a large white wedding, they settled in Sydney, Australia. They had four children, and their descendants still live in Australia today.

Frederick Octavious Prust and his wife Maria Whiter also had twin boys

Shown picture here below when they were in the army in the First World War, they were:

5) **Alfred James Prust** was born in **1891-1977**. He married **Alice Sophia Hooper**; they had no issue. Alfred died in Rugby, Northamptonshire, and

6) Edward Charles Prust was born in **1891-1978.** He married **Ann B Davies**; they also had no issues. Edward also died in Rugby, Northamptonshire.

7) Percy Ernest Prust, **1893-1919,** the youngest of the siblings who died aged 26 years old.

The twins, Alfred and Edward Prust, both became famous artists in the 1930s, showing their paintings at various Exhibitions and at 'The Royal Academy of Art' in London. Although later in life, their professions were as an 'Advertising Artist' and Signwriter.

Frederick Octavius Prust passed away in 1894, aged forty-eight years old, of Rheumatic Fever and Heart Disease. Maria, his wife, was left to raise their children, with their ages ranging from 1 year - 14 years. She worked hard and all hours to earn money as a Machinist and costume maker. Maria died in **1939,** aged 82 years old. Her wishes were to be buried with her youngest son Percy.

The *Youngest Son of Elizabeth Thomas Pascoe and William Thomas Prust*

Theophilus Issiah Prust
1848-1881
Engineer

Elizabeth Arnold
1847-1931

The fourth son of William Thomas and Elizabeth Thomas Prust was Theophilus Isaiah Prust, and he was born at 6 Beauford Place, Bristol, on the 4 January 1848. This is a photograph taken of Theo when he took a trip to visit his aunt Bethulia in Adelaide, Australia, in **1865**. Theo married Elizabeth Arnold in 1870 in Hackney. His occupation was given as an Engine fitter. They went on to have seven children, and all were given the second name of 'Pascoe'.

In **1881** Theo died from Tuberculosis (commonly known as TB) at the young age of 35, leaving seven children under the age of 10 years old, including a baby. His eldest child, a daughter, was called **Elizabeth Pascoe Prust 1871-1946,** named after her grandmother, and she later married **Benjamin Garrett** and had twelve children. Elizabeth was a lifelong socialist and later joined the labour party. She became Hackney's first Mayor in 1942. Elizabeth also served on the Public Health, Maternity, and Child Welfare Committees, and was vice chairman of the Local Savings Committee, the Committee of the Kings Home for Nurses, and Local Employment Committees, plus various other committees. She was also on the board of governors at 'The London Chest Hospital'. Towards the end of her life, she was known as 'GRANDMA DALSTON. Elizabeth died in 1946, aged 75 years old.

William Edward Prust
1867- 1925
Engineer & Cycle maker

Emily Lucy Keeping
1880-1924
Tobacconist kiosk owner

William Edward Prust was the eldest son of William Edward Pascoe and Laura Prust. He was born on the 11th of July **1867** in Bethnal Green, London; this is a reproduction of a picture of a sketch of him on the front pages of a cycling magazine called 'The Ariel Gazette' dated **1893** with William (known as Bill) looking very dapper in his fashionable boater hat and cravat of the time when he was twenty-six years old. There are a few interesting mentions and quotes about the person Bill Prust in this magazine as follows: - *'Bill Prust has the biggest calf in the club',* and the following story.

Setting off on our Velocipedes'

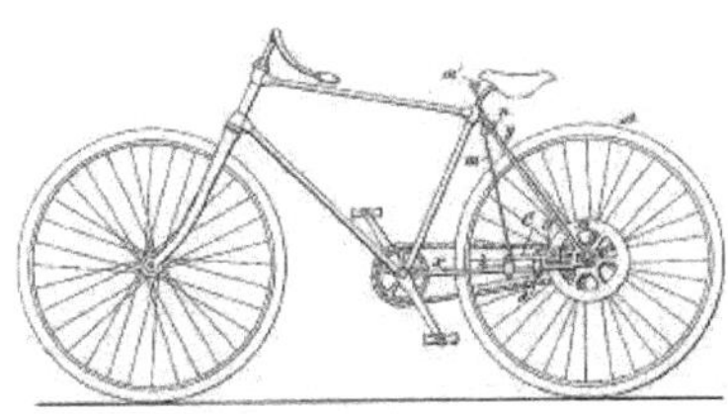

Twenty-five of us started out on our cycles to Southend in Essex and having been misdirected we were all tired and sleepy. We had cycled Forty miles at night, when in vain we sought out a B & B for beds for the night. After knocking on many a door, a face would peep out then vanish and a bolt shot! It would seem that our attire and 'Velocipedes' were too much for the Essex folk. So, we left them, and pulling down some straw from a stack we slept in a field. W. Prust, afraid of thieves roped himself around his cycle and during the night kicked half his spokes out"!

The following article that I found in my research was from a gentleman in Australia whose ancestor was also a member and mentioned in The Ariel Gazette. He kindly sent me a copy of the relevant pages concerning my own ancestor 'William Edward Prust'. This is a translation of the following page: -

Mr William E Prust has been very much amongst the Ariel Prizes this year, and a second in 15-mile Road Handicap in his latest win. Mr Prust's nickname of 'the irrepressible Index' is a sufficient insight into his character. Although his pranks frequently give the club away, he is generally liked, for the hard, toughened, powerful, exterior of the man, is but the shell that enclosed a large soft heart. Does anyone have a puncture; Bill Prust is always behind helping and is ever generous and encouraging to men less speedy than him. Some few years ago, when late one night, a member of 'The Sun' was killed at Woodford, Prust carried the heavy lifeless body half a mile to shelter, and the kind erstwhile noisy dare-devil Bill Prust, felt the terrible mishap as keen as anyone.

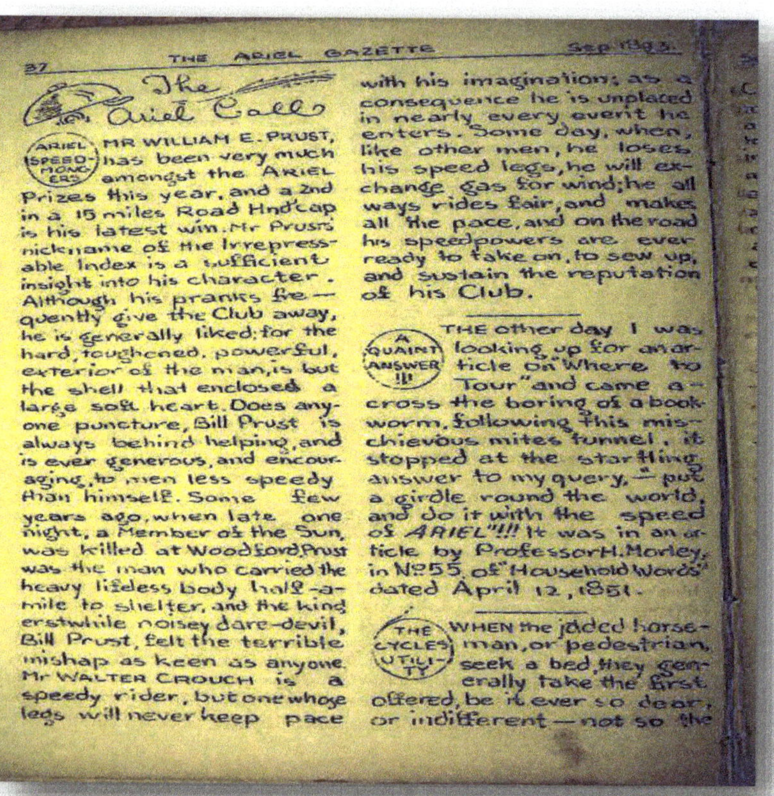

37 THE ARIEL GAZETTE Sep 1893.

The Ariel Call

(ARIEL SPEED-MONGERS) MR WILLIAM E. PRUST, has been very much amongst the ARIEL Prizes this year, and a 2nd in a 15 miles Road Hnd'cap is his latest win. Mr Prust's nickname of the Irrepressable Index is a sufficient insight into his character. Although his pranks frequently give the Club away, he is generally liked: for the hard, toughened, powerful, exterior of the man, is but the shell that enclosed a large soft heart. Does anyone puncture, Bill Prust is always behind helping, and is ever generous, and encouraging, to men less speedy than himself. Some few years ago, when late one night, a Member of the Sun, was killed at Woodford, Prust was the man who carried the heavy lifeless body half-a-mile to shelter, and the kind erstwhile noisey dare-devil, Bill Prust, felt the terrible mishap as keen as anyone. Mr WALTER CROUCH is a speedy rider, but one whose legs will never keep pace with his imagination; as a consequence he is unplaced in nearly every event he enters. Some day, when, like other men, he loses his speed legs, he will exchange gas for wind; he all ways rides fair, and makes all the pace, and on the road his speedpowers are ever ready to take on, to sew up, and sustain the reputation of his Club.

(A QUAINT ANSWER !!!) THE other day I was looking up for an article on "Where to Tour" and came across the boring of a book-worm, following this mischievous mites tunnel, it stopped at the startling answer to my query, "put a girdle round the world, and do it with the speed of ARIEL"!!! It was in an article by Professor H. Morley, in No 55 of "Household Words" dated April 12, 1851.

(THE CYCLES UTILITY) WHEN the jaded horseman, or pedestrian, seek a bed, they generally take the first offered, be it ever so dear, or indifferent — not so the

In **1893** Bill's business was in 'The Motorcycle' trade. Here is an advert written by his hand that he placed in the Gazette at that time. 175, Sandringham Road Dalston, was also the address of the family home where he lived with his parents and siblings.

Note: The Velocipede is the name of an early form of bicycle propelled by working pedals on cranks fitted to the front axle. 'The Sun' was another cycling club in London.

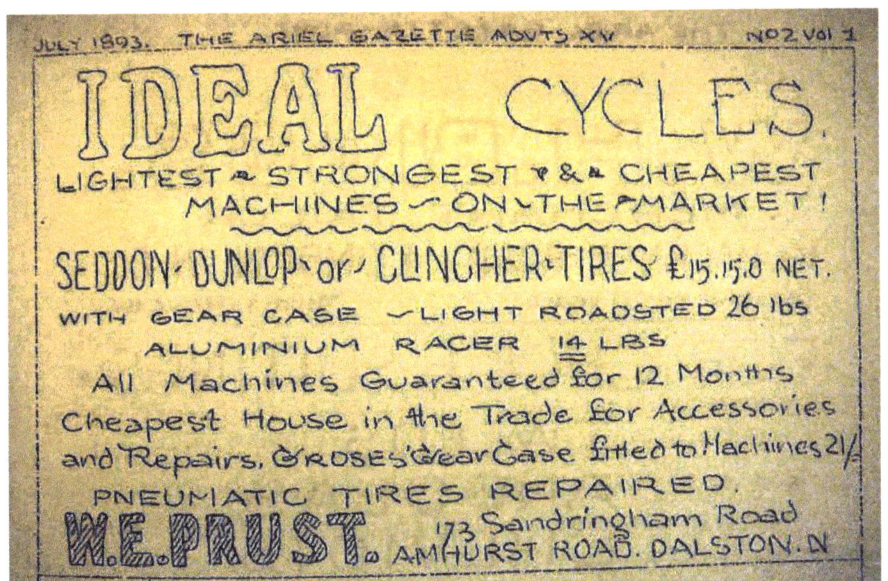

In **1894** Bill won a silver plaque for Cycling from 'The Ariel Cycling Club' shown here below.

1897 Bill was aged thirty years old and had always been known as a ladies' man when he met and wowed a young lady, seventeen-year-old Emily Lucy Keeping, and they got married when Emily was two months pregnant. They married at St. Phillips Church in Dalston. Emily was born in Bournemouth, Hampshire, and her family came from Jersey in the Channel Islands. She was the daughter of George James Keeping, who had the occupation of a tobacconist. William (known as Bill) had the occupation of an Engineer and Cycle maker, and they lived in Bethnal Green and Dalston in Hackney. He built up a thriving family business and was well-known in the Motor trade. He also had other business interests in the area.

Bill and his wife Emily (who was known by the name of 'Cecilia') had their first child, a son who was born in **1897**, whom they called William Edward George Prust. Then one year later, in **1898,** they had a daughter, and they called her Ethel Clara Prust, and in **1900** another daughter was called Florence Clara Cecilia Prust. The marriage wasn't always a happy one, and it is said that Bill was a philanderer! It is known that in later years, Emily Lucy (Cecilia) took to drinking and was known to have an alcohol problem within the family.

This is a letter written by Eileen Grey, who was the granddaughter of Cecilia and the daughter of Ethel Clara Prust

"My grandmother (Emily Lucy Keeping) when she was younger didn't drink and was a very good woman. One of my grandfather's brothers 'Uncle Fred' and his wife both contracted Tuberculosis and died leaving a young son 'Ken', whom my grandmother brought up as her own son. Ken worked in the Post Office when he grew up, but later he also died of TB like his parents. Later in life my grandmother separated from my grandfather. My grandmother moved to Southend and later fell down where building works were carried out and next day she died.
My mother told me that her father was preparing to get married again but her mother who loved him very much vowed he would never marry anyone else.

Six months later my grandfather caught pneumonia and died. The garage was left to the only son Uncle Billy. We were living in Bournemouth then. My grandfather left mother enough money then to buy a car and a drapery business in London, as mum was lonely in Bournemouth and wanted to move back to London, which they did. They bought 48 Dalston Lane which was originally owned by my grandfather Gray on my father's side of the family, his grandmother Louise was a Court Dressmaker and had sixteen girls working for her. She left the business to my grandfather, Auntie Louise, and grandfather's sister. My grandfather owned quite a few shops and an arcade in Dalston Lane, but someone was trying to get one of the shops but because he didn't, grandfather believed he started a fire which destroyed the arcade which being at the back of the railway wasn't insured and he lost all his money in 1916. We are told that he took a whip and whipped the man within an inch of his life."

Below is an advert found in The Mercury Newspaper in May **1904**

PRUST BROS.
CYCLE & MOTOR ENGINEERS,
Sandringham Road,
Dalston,
And HIGHBURY CORNER

Motor Repairs by Experienced Workmen
MOTOR-CARS & CYCLES FOR HIRE
Petrol Stored, Grease, Engine Oils
Motor and Cycle Accessories kept in stock
Accumulators charged.
Gent.'s Cycle Built to order - - - £5-5-0
with Free Wheel & Rim Brake.

SEND FOR OUR LIST.
EASY TERMS ARRANGED.

The 1900s was the early age of the Motor Car, although it took a while for the car to make a real social impact. Indeed, it is arguable that the bicycle was a more socially significant invention than the private car. So, in **1904** Bill set up a business called Prust Brothers Ltd., Motorcycle Engineers, with his brother Arthur Watson Prust who was also an engineer and lived in Highbury. The business became extremely profitable, and after a while, Arthur Watson Prust left the business to pursue other business interests as he later opened an off-licence shop on Chatsworth Road in London and lived above the premises. Bill was doing well, so he bought a series of other businesses, and one of them was a tobacconist shop for his wife, Cecilia.

In **1909** his father, William Edward Pascoe Prust, sadly died at his home in Highbury. London. William Edward Prust's occupation at that time, according to the census, was also an Engineer and a Cycle maker first class

In **1911** and **1912,** he continued the business of Prust Bros., Ltd; this was the exciting age of the motor car, so he decided to buy the premises at 4 Dalston Lane, Hackney, and converted the premises into a garage with a forecourt selling petrol with a pump and garage/workshop at the rear. The upstairs of these premises he turned into living accommodation. A telephone was installed, and the number was Dalston 2114, which was quite a considerable invention for the time.

Bill became a well-known and respected garage proprietor with some standing in the local community, employing a few staff to carry out repairs and valeting services for his customers. There were not many cars on the roads in those days, but Bill used to service the cars of the local professional businessman and doctors who were his main clients as they could make many more calls in a working day than otherwise was possible.

For most people on even average incomes, the private car was an impossible dream. Cars were still rare, but although his 'bread and butter' was still the Cycle trade, he had the foresight to know that the age of the car was on the increase. And indeed, that increase was rapid, from 8,000 vehicles in 1905 to 132,000 vehicles travelling on the roads in 1914, at the outbreak of World War One.

In **1919** Bill became a Freemason and was given a large, engraved plaque/ certificate which read: "United Grand Lodge of Ancient Free and Accepted Masons of England". It reads**:**
'To All Whom It May Concern. This is to certify that our brother William Edward Prust, who hath signed his name in the margin hereof, was regularly initiated into Free Masonry on the 15th day of May AL.5918 in the St. John's Lodge No.795 Cookham. Etc

In **1924** Emily left Bill after she found out that he was having an affair with another woman. She went to stay with her daughter Ethel who was married by then and was living in Southend on Sea in Essex. She also got herself a job and found employment at the Post Office in Southend sorting letters. Below is a photograph of The Post office, which is now a pub.

It was here that she met her sad demise as she had an accident and fell down a flight of stairs in the post office. She was taken to the Victoria Hospital in Southend, where she sadly died. An inquest into her death was held on the day after, and it was certified that she died of a 'Fracture of the scull due to an accidental fall'. She was 44 years old.

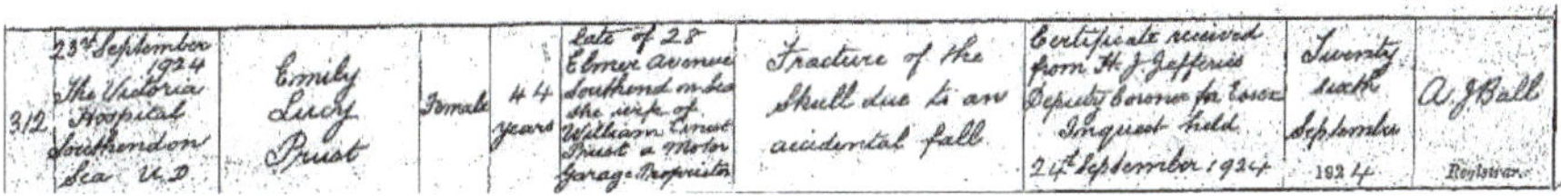

312	23rd September 1924 The Victoria Hospital Southendon Sea U.D	Emily Lucy Prust	Female	44 years	Late of 28 Elmer Avenue Southend on Sea the wife of William Ernest Prust a Motor Garage Proprietor	Fracture of the Skull due to an accidental fall	Certificate received from H. J. Jefferies Deputy Coroner for Essex Inquest held 24th September 1924	Twenty sixth September 1924	A. J Ball Registrar

There is a document from her daughter Ethel that quotes that her father was planning to marry again soon after her mother died, but then he promised her that out of respect for his late wife, he wouldn't re-marry.

1925 just one year later, Bill falls ill and dies in The German Hospital. He was 58 years old. His son William Edward George Prust, was present at his death. The German Hospital (Pictured opposite has now been turned into luxury apartments). William died of heart failure and was buried in Abney Park Cemetery in Stoke Newington, London.

His son William Edward George Prust, known as Bill Prust Junior, then took over the family business and garage in Dalston Lane. This business was left to his three children equally, but his son William Edward George ran it daily. William also left £1,813.17s.9d (worth about £55,000 in today's money) to his two daughters. Executers to the will were Ernest John Tyrie (Clerk), husband of Florence, and Leslie Edmund Grey (Department Manager), husband to Ethel. This just shows that even in the 1920s, women were not in charge of their own inheritance. Here is a photograph of the three children of William Edward Prust and his wife, Emily Lucy Keeping

From left to right: Ethel Clara Prust 1898-1974, Florence Clara Cecilia Prust 1900-1986 and William Edward George Prust 1897-1974.

20th Century London Prust's

William Edward George Prust
1897-1974
The garage owner,

Ada b. Brinkworth
1896-1987
A Lady

William Edward George Prust, also known as 'Bill', was born on the 10th of October **1897**. He was the eldest child and only son of William Edward & Emily Lucy Prust. He married **Ada Beatrice Brinkworth** in Islington in March **1916.** He was 18 years old, and she was 19 years old. Ada was also pregnant when she married Bill, and she was the daughter of Henry Thomas Brinkworth, an accounts collector and Alice Maud Dutton. They lived in the large accommodation above the garage in Dalston Lane inherited from his father and employed one maid named 'Violet'. It was told that when this maid left her to employ, she stole some family silver!

Bill studied to become an Engineer like his father and took over the family business in Dalston in **1919** after his father retired when he was just 22 years old. There were few motor cars on the road in those times, but business was thriving as there were even fewer garages that sold petrol.

Shown below is a picture of Bill with his treasured motor car. This car was left to him in a will of the family Doctor, Doctor Thomas Haig, in 1952 when he passed away.

As well as his business Bill became involved with the German Hospital (where his beloved father died). This hospital was situated just up the road from where Bill and his family lived in Dalston Lane, above the garage. Bill did quite a lot of business with the German hospital and often chauffeured the doctors around when their cars went in his garage for repairs. His dealing with 'The German Hospital' grew. Indeed, in a bid to increase business, he even told doctors and administrators of the German hospital that he was of German descent! Which was utter nonsense, but as word got around the local area, Ada, on occasion, was refused by the local shopkeepers to buy her food even though she had the ration coupons and money to buy it. She later said that some food they had to purchase on the black market, this was obviously in Wartime 1939-1945, and the government proclaimed that all German nationals would be interred in a camp on the Isle of Wight. So in **1939,** Bill was visited at the family home by the government's MI5 with a view to internment (having a German-sounding name and close links with The German Hospital), so Bill had

to prove that he was English which he quickly did so. He later became an ARP in the war due to the increased enemy bombing during the Blitz on London. In World War Two, the ARP was created. Whereby Men were asked to join up to help with the managing of Air Raid Sirens and directing people to the shelters etc. One night bombing was bad, and he was escorting his niece Eileen to the shelter when he forgot his helmet they both went back for it, and a bomb dropped exactly where they would have been standing. Bill threw Eileen down and threw himself on top of her to save her from the blast! So, the story is told that going back for his hat saved both their lives!

Bill was like his father and had an eye for other women, which caused the fiery red-haired Ada some concerns. It is known that she caught him with a lady and blacked his eye on just one occasion.

Bill and Ada both loved music and would often listen to the legendary 'Vera Lynn' on the wireless. They had a piano in their living room which Ada used to play, and Bill used to sing along to.
They loved going to the Theatre and often went to 'The Hackney Empire', especially if 'Max Miller' was on the program as he was a great favourite and as they knew each other socially Ada and Bill got the best seats in the house.

The Children of Bill and Ada Prust

Bill & Ada had four children; their first child was a daughter

1) Irene E.E. Prust b. **1916-1918**, who sadly died aged just 18 months old.
One year later, she gave birth to another daughter

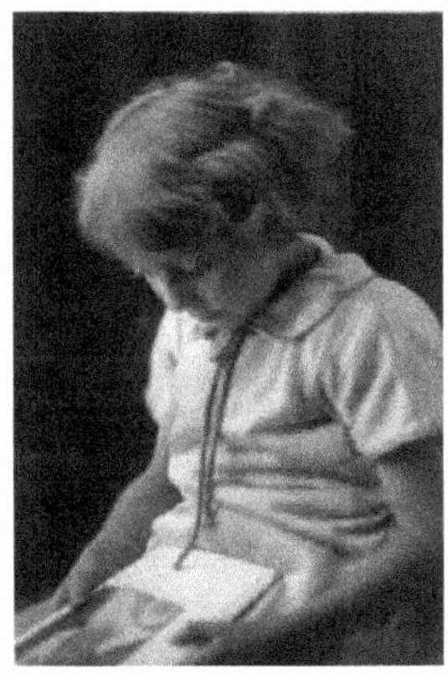

2) Vera E Prust 1919-2018 she was born on 'Valentines' Day' February 14th, 1919. This photograph on the left is of Vera as a child. Vera married twice; her first husband was **Leslie Downey,** from **1917-1988** (this marriage was later annulled). Her second husband was **Ralph William Palmer, 1923-1999.** His occupation was a Sergeant in the police force, and later, he worked for the Bank of England. They had no children.

3) Jean Constance Prust 1925-2019. Shown on the left on her wedding day in September 1941 when she was just 16 years old. Jean married three times, first to a handsome, dashing Grenadier Guardsman called **Frank Douglas Cecil Barnet (1920-1943**), aged 22 years old. Their daughter Valerie was born in **1942**. In **1943** when their daughter was only eight months old, Frank, who was on leave from the army, died, leaving the devastated young mother, Jean, a widow at just eighteen years old. Shown here below is Jean in the uniform of the Norwegian Army in about 1944 when she was just 19

years old. One year later, in **1944,** Jean meets a young Norwegian sailor called **Odd Vennesland** and marries him. Jean took her young daughter and went with her husband back to Norway and forthwith joined the Norwegian army. The marriage broke down, and she divorced Odd and went back to England with her young daughter. Shown here on the left is a photo of Jean and her second husband, Odd Vennesland.

In 1947 Jean met another young man just out of the army, and he became her third husband, **Brian Mills**. The couple had two children together, and Brian adopted Jean's daughter Valerie.

This marriage also ended in divorce. Brian Mills died in 2015. Jean died in 2019, and their daughter Valerie (as she was known) died in Germany in 2022.

The Wedding photo of Jean & Brian Mills

c. **1930.** Below is an old family photo of Vera, her sister Jean, and their cousin Eileen Ethel Grey when they were children in a ballet troupe. Vera is on the end right (the tallest girl, Jean, six years younger, is on the left, and their cousin Eileen is third from the left.

4) **William Edward Prust 1926-2011** Born on the 25 July **1926** (He was known as Bill Jnr.) Bill went to the local primary school in Hackney, where he met another pupil who he was later to marry. He left school at fourteen years old. His first job was in a factory marking leather bags, and the wages were twenty shillings a week (one pound). Bill had a variety of jobs after leaving school, but the longest one was as a shop assistant, and he soon found he had 'The gift of the gab'. He lasted two years in that job before he decided to join the army just one month after his eighteenth birthday. Bill enlisted in the Army in August **1944.** He had driving experience due to driving his father's car and had experience as an Electrical Engineer also due to his father's business. He was eighteen, 5'7", and weighed just eight stone 7 inches. He was recommended by his commanding officer to be a 'Rifleman', but Bill wasn't really army material as he kept going absent without leave.

Elsie Tasker

Bill left the Army in August **1945** when he was 19 years old and married 18-year-old **Elsie Tasker,** his childhood sweetheart, in February **1946**. Their first child, a daughter, was born five months later. Another child, a daughter, was born nine years later. Bill and Elsie later divorced in 1958. Bill also had a son by a partner in 1962. Bill's second wife was **June Rosemary Scott** 1940-2002, by whom he had three children.

Holy Trinity Primary School, Hackney, London. Pictured middle, back row, Bill Prust, pictured front row, second from left, his childhood sweetheart Elsie Tasker, whom he later married.

2006 Bill at his 80th birthday party in Southend on Sea, Essex.

Ethel Clara Cecilia Prust 1898-1974

Ethel at her daughter's wedding.

The second child of William Edward Prust and his wife, Emily Lucy Keeping, was Ethel Clara Cecilia Prust 1898-1974. A picture of Ethel is shown here. Ethel married **Leslie Edmund Gray** from **1897-1979.** Ethel was born in Hackney. She married Leslie Grey in **1921** in Dalston, Hackney. They had four children. Mary Grey **1924-2001**. Eileen Grey **1922-1955**. Peter Grey **1930-2011**, and Barbara Gray in **1932**-.

Ethel died in Southend on Sea on 15 April **1974,** aged **75** years sadly, outliving her daughter Eileen who died at the young age of 33 years, leaving a husband and two young children called Janice & Howard Howell both now deceased. By courtesy of Janice's daughter, below is a family photo on the beach of Ethel with her two daughters, Mary and Eileen in Ramsgate, Kent in 1935.

Ethel with two of her daughters at Ramsgate in 1935

Florence Laura Prust 1900-1986.

Florence Laura Prust on her wedding day.

Florence Laura Prust was the third child of William Edward & Emily Lucy Prust, **1900-1986**. She was born in November 1900. She married **Ernest John Tyrie 1894-1969** at St. Philips Church, Dalston, on 13th August **1921**. He was the son of George Tyrie, a Brush Manufacturer. They moved to Westcliff on Sea, Essex and lived there all their lives. Florence became a keen golfer and won many ladies' championships. They had no children.

THESE ARE THE FAMILY BRANCHES OF THE PRUST FAMILY THAT I HAVE RESEARCHED UP TO THE PRESENT TIME. IF YOU HAVE ANYTHING TO ADD, PLEASE LET ME KNOW AT: smallwoodjean@yahoo.co.uk.

Names of people mentioned in this book are on the following pages:

Ackland p.56. Addams, p.115,122. Arnold p.173. Arundell p.12,15,16.

Ashton p. 89. Atkins p.37,142. Anderton p.54,58. Annesley p.66.

Bagenhole p.45. Balhatchet p.75. Balthis p.82. Barter p.167. Barnett p.185. Banyo p.140. Beaufort p.44. Bear p.85. Beattie p.167. Beer p.85. Blagdon p.56. Bowman p.84,91. Boleyn p.13. Borovikorsky p.19. Box p.142. Bragg p.55. Brinkworth p.182. Brown p.92. Budd p.74. Burgh p.88. Burnard p.91. Burrows p.93. Bush 134.

Carey p.56,58. Carnsewe p.54. Castieau p.141. Cavill p.112. Champney p.37. Ching p. 75, 81. Chope p.15. Christie p.118. Clevedon p.55. Cloutman p.84, 91. Coard p.138. Courtenay p.14,27,36,50. Cobin p.24. Coffin p.59. Collings p.37. Cooper p.54. Corydon p.37. Cromwell p.13,15,109. Cruse p.91. Curtis p.114.

Davies p. 112,113,172. De Rossi p.119. Defoe p.7. Dey p.12. Docton p.125. Downey p.185. Drake p.50. Drew p.49, 136,138. Du Bois p.67. Dynham p.7, 17.

Ellacottn p.93. Elston p.71. Ellis p.75 Escott p.128.

Fish p.91. Fitzwarren p.12.

Galsworthy p.72, 75. Gooding p.139. Grey p.181, 189. Grossmith p.28. Gyntha p.18, 30.

Hamlyn p.85,90. Harris p.83,84,89. Hayes p. 111. Holman p. 46,57. Hooper p.74,172. Hudson p.116. Hunt p.12.

Jenkins p.81. Jewell p.55. Jose p.98.

Keeping p.167, 174. Keyes, Keho p. 138. King p.84. King Arthur p.50. King Edward I p.36, 40, 43. King Harold p.75

King Henry VIII p.11. King Richard II p.43. King William I. p.44 Kirkland p. 167.

Lang p. 56. Lendon 72,76. Leigh p. 65. Littlejohn p. 73. Lloyd p.112. Luttrell p. 11,19,44.

Mann p. 171. Medland p.91,110. Miles, Moffet p.139. Moulton p.51. Mugford p. 72,84.

Nelson p. 88. Newcourt p. 49. Orchard p. 11, 25. Otterbourne p. 106.

Palmer p.185. Pascoe p.150, 154, 159, 161. Pauline/Pawline p.57,91. Perrot p.17. Pillman p.76. Pollard p.17. Pincombe p. 60. Pope p.14,15. Pyke p.111.

Queen Elizabeth I, p.17,18. Quicke p.49.

Randell p.98. Rowe p.74, 76,81. Riley p.81. Ruffley p.118.

Sage p.139. Scott, p.187. Silke p. 86. Slater p.130. Stevens p.114. Stewart p.95. Stone 50,76. Stuckley p.25. Stapleton p.38,40. Sterte p. p. 51.

Tasker p. 187. Turner p.81. Turbow p.38,40. Tyrie p.191

Velly p.25. Venisland p. 185. Verstoosky p. 118. Vigurs p.71. Vine p.57, 73, 74.

Walker p. 105, 106. Way p. 92. Welbourne p.108. Whiter p.171. Wilberforce p.102,102. Wills p.97. Wood p. 49. Woodbine/Woolbine p. 103. Wythecombe p. 51. Yeo p. 60. Zouche p.12.

These people facing common strife
Passing through this world of life
Their stories need to be written
Their stories need to be told
So the history of our ancestor
We pass down to the children of our fold

Here on earth they walked upon its face
In bygone years and a bygone place
The times of yesteryear we are blind
Dissolution, revolutions, religious fervour
And the kind.

But one thing we have in common
Is love, happiness, joy and pain
These emotions we feel the same
What we are it is believed
Comes from the DNA of our genes
Another generation, another life
We face together that common strife.

Jeanette Prust Smallwood

www.ingramcontent.com/pod-product-compliance
Ingram Content Group UK Ltd.
Pitfield, Milton Keynes, MK11 3LW, UK
UKHW062302290726
14090UKWH00017B/844